The Blue Book

By J.C. Bard

The following is the first draft of a textbook in progress that is composed of class handouts, original writings, and Open AI sourced generic introductions. The key term definitions and quotes came from a variety of sources, including but not limited to Wikipedia, Open AI, Goodreads, and Webster's online dictionary.

Chapter 1: Writing

"I was a late bloomer. But anyone who blooms at all, ever, is very lucky. "

— Sharon Olds

"The most essential gift for a good writer is a built-in, shockproof, crap detector. This is the writer's radar and all great writers have had it."

–Ernest Hemingway

As a writing instructor, I am constantly thinking about questions, such as, "What is the purpose of writing?" and "What is the best way to teach writing?" The answers to these questions are constantly evolving over time, though some things do remain constant. In regard to the first question, I believe that writing is the way we think through ideas, hone them, and ultimately articulate our thoughts about the world and our place in it. With the proliferation of artificial intelligence and large language models such as Chat GPT, and Bard, the issue seems to be complicated a bit, but I don't think it changes the essence of writing as a tool for thinking and self-definition. But, given the capabilities of AI, I understand how a student might think: *If I can have AI write something for me, what is the purpose of even learning how to write?* It is a good question, and one that I continue to think about a lot, even as I write this paragraph from the contents of my own brain, and revise it to make it more cogent and precise.

The first answer to this question comes from the idea that writing and thinking are the same thing. In other words, one could just as easily pose the question: *If I can get a computer to think for me, what is the point of learning how to think?* Here, I believe it is easier to see how problematic the issue is for students and humanity at large. One of the main reasons why I went to college was to become a better thinker, and problem solver. There is a lot of information that I learned and forgot, but at the same time I learned the process of learning, how to work with others, how to ask questions and find answers. This ability transcends the academic setting to both our professional and personal lives, and cannot be replaced by machines but can be augmented by them.

Imagine if one relied upon a computer to think for them at all times. On a personal level, one is letting a computer define them, colonize their brains, to make them whatever the computer or algorithm thinks they should be. "Siri, what is my favorite color?" Similarly, on a professional level, it could mean not being able to contribute anything original or insightful to your team because you don't have any thinking skills. There is a very funny video I saw once entitled something like, "The first day of trial for a lawyer who got through college using AI to do all his homework." You can imagine how well this individual performed in court as he struggled to understand questions with a blank look on his face. This was a funny exaggeration of a very real truth. Writing and thinking are both skills that require practice in order to become fluent in them, and the less you practice, the less well you will perform at these tasks. This also reminds me of a quote I once read that said something to the effect of, "There is nothing worth having that doesn't require work to obtain." In other words, if a student is paying to go to college and learn skills, and they have AI perform all of those skills for them, it would be like taking a karate class and having a robot fight for you. What happens the day you actually need to fight? Or perform well in an interview, etc.?

To be fair, there will be a time and place for using AI. I have written the first draft of this textbook with the help of AI, for example, but if I had not already done the work of learning how to write and think, (A) I wouldn't know what I needed help with writing and (B) the disjunct between my own skills as a writer and the skill of AI would be so glaringly obvious as to be laughable. In other words, the more skill you have, the better you will be able to implement AI to your advantage.

In regard to the second question, which is, "What is the best way to teach writing?" I am still working on this, but I have discovered some key strategies that seem to help.

1) Break down writing into smaller parts, so that students can have success with a paragraph before having to write a ten page paper.

2) Break down the different kinds of paragrapTEhs so that students know what the point of each paragraph is, such as a summary, narrative, expository, etc.

3) Give examples of each kind of writing for students to look at and reverse engineer into their own paragraphs.

4) Utilize templates and key phrases to help with formulaic writing, such as the kind GPT excels.

5) Use AI to perform the most mundane of tasks, such as creating a works cited page, so that the majority of a

student's energy is focused on critical thinking and analytical skills.

Everything I have just written is from personal experience, self-inquiry, critical thinking with myself and others, and reading. I understand what I am saying, and could articulate further on any point if needed. This would not be the case, however, if I had simply asked AI to tell me what the point of writing is. I might be able to parrot what it says, but without doing the intellectual work, I would soon find myself out of my depth, and grasping for straws. Below I have asked AI to write me an introduction to writing and why it is important. Indeed, it contains many of the themes I have already spoken about. But I also read it over and edited it to make sure what it says is in-line with my own vision and goals. This is how AI can be used collaboratively in a productive way, but also notice how I have given AI credit where credit is due, so that one will not be accused of plagiarism.

In this book, I have put together the key terms, and ideas, and quotes that are critical to becoming a better writer and critical thinker. The primary goal of this course will equip you with the tools to express yourself with clarity, creativity, and confidence. In order to achieve this, we will explore the power of words and how they shape our thoughts, ideas, and interactions. Through various writing assignments, discussions, and analysis of diverse texts, we delve into the intricacies of crafting compelling arguments, structuring coherent essays, and engaging readers through persuasive rhetoric. This course aims to enhance your ability to learn new material, articulate your thoughts and perspectives in a variety of genres, from informative essays to persuasive arguments and personal narratives. You'll learn how to conduct research, evaluate sources, and incorporate evidence effectively to support your ideas. We'll also explore the principles of organization, coherence, and style to help you create well-structured and engaging compositions. A lot of people have a fear of writing because they think it is about perfect grammar and punctuation, but this is only one aspect of writing that should only be emphasized in terms of clarity of ideas (Open AI).

I agree with everything the above paragraph says, but it also reveals one of AI's biggest flaws, which is how generalized the writing is. Sure, everything is grammatically correct and sounds good on paper, but there are no specific examples or elucidations of what is meant by "compelling arguments" or "coherent essays," which is where I will be required to give more specific examples. Moreover, as the next paragraphs will illustrate, I need to have the ability to write as well as AI in order to use it as my co-creator.

I wrote the following, but to be honest, I sound like a robot even to myself.

In addition to improving your writing, this class will also nurture your critical thinking skills by encouraging you to analyze, interpret, and synthesize information from various sources. We'll delve into different rhetorical strategies, logical fallacies, and methods of persuasion, allowing you to develop a keen eye for effective writing and the tools to critically evaluate the works of others. Learning how to learn and vocabulary building will also be an essential part of this class as it is the basis for gaining mastery of any subject.

Collaborative activities and peer feedback will be integral parts of this course, fostering an environment where you can learn from and with your fellow students. By engaging in constructive discussions, you'll expand your perspectives and refine your ideas, ultimately becoming a more proficient communicator.

Beyond the formal aims of this course, what I am ultimately trying to do is give you an overall introduction to academic culture, so that you you can leave this class with a basic understanding of some of the major issues that you will be faced with, both in life and college, such as the role of capitalism, technology, and critical thinking. These issues should be familiar to you on some level, but depending on the quality of your secondary education, there will be a wide variety of skills and fluency, and my aim is to give everyone a challenge wherever they are on this spectrum, so that you will leave this class with a higher level of intellectual confidence than you came in with. Education, of course, is a lifelong journey, and my hope also is that this will continue to inspire you to know more about the world, and the critical issues that affect us all.

"If you separate the writing process into two stages, you can exploit these opposing muscles one at a time: first be loose and accepting as you do fast early writing; then be critically tough minded as you revise what you have produced. What you'll discover is that these two skills used alternately don't undermine each other at all, they enhance each other.``

— Peter Elbow, Writing With Power: Techniques for Mastering the Writing Process

As I said earlier, one of the key strategies for learning, is knowing the vocabulary needed to understand any given subject, and since we are one the subject of writing, here are some key terms and concepts you will need to know:

The writing process is different for everyone, but there are some important concepts you should know that have helped me a lot on my journey as a writer:

The first idea is that there are basically two stages in the writing process, what I would call freewriting and then revision.

Free writing: Free writing is a technique used to generate ideas or overcome writer's block by allowing the writer to write continuously without concern for grammar, structure, or logic. It involves setting a time limit and writing whatever comes to mind, without editing or self-censorship.

Outlining: Coming up with the basic ideas of your paper before you embark on writing it.

Revision is the process of reviewing, modifying, and refining a written work to improve its clarity, coherence, organization, and effectiveness. It involves rethinking and restructuring ideas, addressing inconsistencies, enhancing the flow of the writing, and ensuring that the intended message is communicated effectively.

Though grammar and punctuation are important, I am most concerned with your ability to articulate your ideas clearly and effectively. I don't need you to sound like a robot, but I want to understand what you're saying.

Breakdown of length of assignments, according to what I ask for; these are rough guidelines but try to keep to them as best you can. Writing concisely is actually harder than writing long form because you are forced to really make every sentence count.

Short answer = 1 to 5 ish complete sentences

Short paragraph = ½ ish page

Long paragraph = 1 ish page

Mini-essay = 1 - 2 ish pages

Full essay = 4-5 ish pages

Examples of Writing:

When I was learning how to write, I was overwhelmed by all the different kinds of writing, so I have tried to break down here the basic styles you will find so that you can better understand what each form is useful for, and what it sounds like. One of the best ways to learn how to write is to reverse engineer what somebody else has written.

    A **narrative** is writing with the primary purpose of telling a story. Here is an example:

    As a college student, my journey to learn how to write has been an exhilarating roller coaster ride of self-discovery and growth. When I first stepped foot into the university, I was filled with a sense of anticipation and excitement, but also a nagging fear of the writing challenges that lay ahead. The first few weeks were a blur of lectures, readings, and assignments. I remember staying up all night to memorize some key terms for my biology class, but forgot them by the test because I was so exhausted. I soon realized that writing in college demanded more than just regurgitating information from textbooks, and getting a good night's sleep. It also required critical thinking, analysis, and the ability to present arguments with clarity and conviction. The expectations were high, and I felt a wave of uncertainty wash over me. Determined to conquer my writing insecurities, I sought guidance from professors, attended writing workshops, and spent countless hours in the campus library immersing myself in books on writing techniques. I was determined to master the art of crafting compelling arguments and expressing myself effectively on the page (Open AI).

(Can you write a transitional phrase between these two paragraphs?)

I hated reading novels when I was younger. I had a hard time focusing for long periods of time, so I would frequently get Cliffsnotes, which were basically summaries of the novel along with some literary analysis. There was one class, however, where the book assigned was "Germinal " by Emile Zola, and there were no Cliffsnotes for this particular novel, so I made up my mind to read it. I remember drinking so much coffee I was shaking as I read the back corner of the library, shifting between pages and looking out the window at the gray sky. I remember it was about horrible working conditions in France, and a revolution that took place. The details are sketchy since this was over 30 years ago, but I do remember one scene where somebody's head is cut off and paraded down the streets of Paris on a stick. I also remember being very proud of myself for actually reading the book, and still consider it a feat, even though I've gone on to read many novels since then. Reflecting on this now, I realize that I have almost no memory of any of the Cliffnotes I read. At best I can remember the basic plot, but I have no emotional memory of the material. It's just blank inside me whereas the novels I actually read like the *Catcher in the Rye*, stuck with me on a deeper level as I related to the main character and his struggles. This has led me to believe that there are two kinds of reading, the first is **informational** where we just want to know the facts, and the second is **experiential** where we want to experience something. To have an experience is such a vague concept, yet we crave it all the time in movies, songs, and books. Imagine reading Cliff Notes for your favorite song instead of listening to it. Sounds absurd right? Yet why is it so different from reading a poem or novel?

Expository writing is a type of writing that aims to explain, inform, or describe a particular topic or concept in a clear, concise, and logical manner. Below is an example about how writing helps critical thinking skills:

      Writing plays a vital role in developing and enhancing critical thinking skills. Through the act of writing, individuals are prompted to organize their thoughts, evaluate information, and construct coherent arguments. Writing encourages individuals to engage in deeper analysis, explore different perspectives, and communicate their ideas effectively. When we put pen to paper or fingers to keyboard, we are forced to clarify our thoughts, examine the validity of our assumptions, and critically evaluate the evidence at hand. There is only so much information we can process without writing it down, and we are limited by the scope of our memory, but writing ideas down allows for a much more comprehensive look at our thoughts and ideas. Writing fosters a disciplined thought process that requires logical reasoning, evidence-based arguments, and the ability to anticipate counterarguments. It enables individuals to express complex ideas, identify gaps in their knowledge, and refine their understanding through research and exploration. Ultimately, writing serves as a catalyst for intellectual growth, empowering individuals to think critically, communicate effectively, and participate actively in the world of ideas. (Open AI)

(Can you write a transitional phrase between these two paragraphs?)

I used to think writing was about showing off, and that the more fancy words I could shove down my reader's throat the better, so that if I said, "In this essay, we will deconstruct the ideological contradictions in T.S. Eliot's "The Waste Land," as it vacillates between a celebration and condemnation of the dominant cultural paradigms that served as the poet's milieu." This writing now reminds me of artificial intelligence in its high diction and somewhat pompous posturing, but sometimes an assignment will require it, but don't think this is the *sine qua non* of good writing. What I am mostly looking for is simply a clarity of ideas. I want to understand, as efficiently as possible, what is being said. Of course, there is a time and a place for higher levels of diction, according to what level of expertise your audience has. Most expository writing that is consumed by readers isn't written in a highly specialized vocabulary. In fact, I think taking things that are complex and being able to articulate them in a more accessible manner is an art unto itself. A lot of academic writing, for me, is the act of translating something from my normal speaking voice such as, "I like the way that the poem "The Waste Land" is both a celebration and critique of modern society to the more formal: "In this essay, we will deconstruct the ideological contradictions in T.S. Eliot's "The Waste Land," as it vacillates between a celebration and condemnation of the dominant cultural paradigms that served as the poet's milieu."`

In order to do this, however, it is imperative that you have a larger vocabulary; hence, the copious inclusion of key terms.

Compare and contrast:

Another example of expository writing is called comparison and contrast, which simply means you are comparing and contrasting two ideas or things to show what they have in common and how they are different. Below is an example:

Capitalism and communism are two distinct economic and political ideologies that have shaped the world's history and continue to influence societies today. Capitalism is an economic system characterized by private ownership of the means of production and a focus on individual profit-seeking. A lemonade stand competes with another lemonade stand across the street to see who can make the most profits while providing refreshment to the consumer. In contrast, communism advocates for collective ownership of the means of production and the abolition of private property, aiming for a classless society where wealth and resources are distributed equally among all citizens. In this neighborhood, everybody would own the lemonade stand, and there would be no profits, only lemonade for all, "each according to their need." While capitalism fosters competition and innovation, encouraging economic growth and technological advancements, communism seeks to eliminate social and economic inequalities, promoting solidarity and cooperation among people. In a capitalist system, there would be incentive, for example, to find better and more efficient ways to produce lemonade for increased profit, while in a communist system, there would have to be other incentives besides profit. However,

Capitalism's inherent tendency towards income inequality and potential exploitation of workers has been a source of criticism, whereas communism's centralized control and lack of individual incentives have been criticized for stifling individual freedoms and curbing entrepreneurial spirit. The debate between capitalism and communism remains a central aspect of global political discourse, with various countries adopting different blends of these ideologies to shape their economic and social structures. (AI)

How could you make the aforementioned paragraph more specific?

How to write a comparison and contrast essay:

Choose two ideas, concepts, characters, etc. that you are going to compare and contrast.

Define them for yourself and the reader

Identify Similarities: Instruct students to identify and list the similarities between the two concepts. These can include shared ideas, goals, motivations.

Identify Differences: Identify and list the differences between the two ideas. These can include contrasting beliefs, behaviors, or attitudes that set them apart from each other.

Organize the Paragraph: Structure the compare and contrast paragraph. You can begin with an introduction that introduces what will be compared and contrasted and also provides some context. Then, give an example of how these things are similar and how they are different. Finally, a conclusion can summarize the main points. For a longer assignment, you would simply give more examples.

Make sure to give support to your comparisons and contrasts with specific evidence from the text. This could include quotes, scenes, or examples that illustrate the shared traits or distinct behaviors.

Use Transitional Phrases: Emphasize the importance of using appropriate transitional phrases (e.g., "similarly," "in contrast," "both," "while," "unlike," etc.) to smoothly guide readers through the comparison and contrast process.

In class assignment: write a short compare and contrast paragraph for one of the following:

Using a Pen vs. Pencil:
Reading Physical Books vs. E-books:
Fast Food vs. Homemade Meals:
Video game of —-----vs. Reality of —----------

Another form of expository writing is called definition, which simply means you are going to define a concept or idea for your reader in more depth/ Below is an example of defining what is called a liberal arts education.

Definition:

The Humanities

The humanities are academic disciplines that study aspects of human society and culture. They use methods that are primarily analytical, critical, or speculative, as distinguished from the mainly empirical approaches of the natural and social sciences. The humanities include the study of ancient and modern languages, literature, philosophy, history, archaeology, anthropology, human geography, law, politics, religion, and art. Scholars in the humanities are often interested in questions that pertain to human experiences, values, ideas, and creative expressions throughout history. These subjects are often considered to be the core of a liberal arts education and are valued for their ability to teach critical thinking, cultural understanding, and communication skills, among other competencies. They can offer unique insights into the human condition and enrich our understanding of the complex and diverse nature of human experiences, fostering empathy, ethical understanding, and a more nuanced perspective on the world (Open AI).

Here are two powerful quotes that explain why the humanities matter:

I am a survivor of a concentration camp. My eyes saw what no person should witness: gas chambers built by learned engineers. Children poisoned by educated physicians. Infants killed by trained nurses. Women and babies shot by high school and college graduates.

So, I am suspicious of education.

My request is this: Help your children become human. Your efforts must never produce learned monsters, skilled psychopaths or educated Eichmanns. Reading, writing, and arithmetic are important only if they serve to make our children more human.

–Haim Ginott

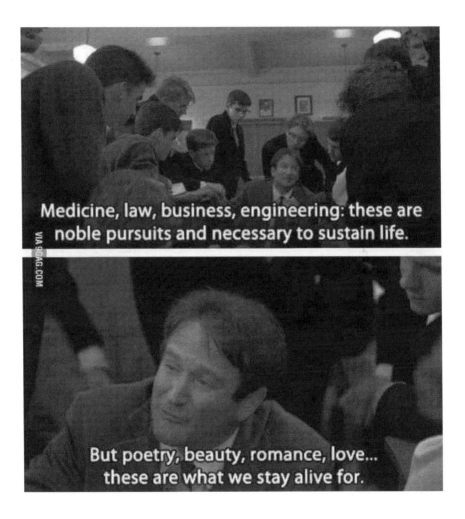

The above meme is taken from the film "The Dead Poet's Society," which is the story of how a teacher at a fancy prep-school played by Robin Williams tries to help his students to live more authentic lives in the face of the expectations of society.

How to write a paragraph of definition or define a concept or term that is important in the subject you are studying. This exercise will not only enhance your understanding of the topic but also improve their ability to communicate complex ideas concisely and accurately.

Here's a step-by-step breakdown of how to do a definition assignment:

Select the Term or Concept: Depending on the subject being taught, choose a term or concept that is essential but might have multiple interpretations or nuances. For example, in a literature class, you could have students define "irony," or in a science class, they could define "photosynthesis."

Research and Study: Research and study the term thoroughly. Explore different definitions from credible sources such as textbooks, scholarly articles, or reputable websites.

Narrow Down the Definition: Analyze the various definitions they found and identify the core elements of the term. Focus on the essential characteristics that define the concept.

Provide Context: Consider the context in which the term is commonly used and how it relates to the broader subject matter.

Understanding the term's context helps in crafting a comprehensive definition.

Craft the Definition Paragraph: Write a well-structured paragraph that introduces the term and provides a clear and concise definition. Use your own language and try to be as clear as possible

Make sure to include examples or scenarios to illustrate the application of the defined term. Examples help reinforce understanding and make the definition more relatable.

In class assignment: Write a paragraph about a word or phrase that you use often, and explain to the reader where you learned it, what it means, and give an example of how you might specifically use this word in context.

Analysis:

Another type of expository writing is an analysis; This is a systematic and detailed examination of something in order to understand its components, structure, behavior, or underlying principles. It involves breaking down a complex topic or subject into its various parts and studying them to gain insights, draw conclusions, or make interpretations. Here is an overview of an analysis of the causes of Wealth Inequality.

Wealth inequality in America is a multifaceted issue with various underlying causes. One of the significant contributors is the disparity in income distribution, where high-earning individuals and corporations accumulate vast amounts of wealth, leaving a large portion of the population with limited resources. This is often exacerbated by regressive tax policies and loopholes that disproportionately benefit the wealthy who are able to use offshore accounts to avoid paying taxes while utilizing the infrastructure paid for by the taxpayer such as the police and road maintenance. Moreover, the decline of unions and weakened labor rights have led to stagnating wages for the working class, while executive compensation and profits for corporations have soared. Additionally, the rising cost of education and healthcare, coupled with limited access to affordable housing, hinders upward mobility for many Americans, further widening the wealth gap. Furthermore, historical factors, such as the legacy of systemic racism and discrimination, have also played a significant role in perpetuating wealth disparities among different racial and ethnic groups. Addressing wealth inequality requires comprehensive policy interventions focused on progressive taxation, strengthening labor rights, improving access to education and healthcare, and tackling systemic biases to create a more equitable society. (AI)

Here is a counter argument to the above paragraph written by AI; look at the transitional phrase that takes us from one topic to the next:

While wealth inequality is often considered a significant concern, some argue that it might not be the most crucial factor to consider in evaluating the well-being of a society. They contend that focusing on wealth inequality can divert attention from more pressing issues such as poverty reduction, overall economic growth, and opportunities for upward mobility. From this perspective, what matters more is that everyone has access to the essential resources and opportunities they need to improve their lives, rather than the relative disparities in wealth between different individuals or groups. The emphasis, therefore, should be on creating policies that foster opportunity and alleviate poverty, rather than simply redistributing wealth, as those who are more concerned with wealth inequality might advocate. Critics of focusing on wealth inequality argue that it may lead to policies that stifle innovation, entrepreneurship, and individual initiative, potentially hindering overall economic prosperity.

Can you see any problems with this argument?

Argumentative:

Here is another example of expository writing that is called argumentative; this is the kind of writing that explicitly makes an argument for or against something. One could argue that all writing is an argument such as in the book Everything's An Argument, but some arguments are more explicit than others. Here is an example of an explicit argument:

Even in an era of advanced AI, teaching writing remains essential because it fosters crucial skills that extend beyond mere information processing. Writing empowers individuals to think critically, articulate their thoughts, and express their unique perspectives. It cultivates creativity, empathy, and the ability to engage in nuanced communication. While AI can assist in streamlining certain writing tasks, it cannot replicate the human capacity for emotional depth, originality, and ethical reasoning. Writing education equips individuals with the tools to navigate complex ideas, advocate for change, and contribute meaningfully to society. By teaching writing, we ensure that individuals develop the essential skills necessary to navigate the world, adapt to evolving technologies, and engage in human connections that go beyond the capabilities of AI (Open AI).

Many of the paragraphs above, though well written in terms of grammar and punctuation, and giving an overview of the topics, still lack what I like to call **specific examples**. Specific examples take us from generalizing about a topic to showing exactly what we are talking about, and to me they make the difference between weak and powerful writing in every kind of writing.

Specific examples:

If I were to ask you, for instance, to give me a specific example of how self-awareness has helped you in some capacity, and I give you a definition of self-awareness as: 1. conscious knowledge of one's own character, feelings, motives, and desires. As in:

"the process can be painful but it leads to greater self-awareness"

A common answer a high school student might give is: "I use self-awareness all the time, and it helps me to function better at work." The End.

Oh boy.

This isn't a specific example; this is what I call "a vague generalization," and we use these all the time when we are talking to people because we assume they don't want any more details before we bore them. In this writing class, however, we need more specific examples for the following reasons:

It gives concrete evidence to support your thesis

It helps to really demonstrate your understanding of key concepts.

It gives you a chance to actually make an intellectual discovery about the subject, instead of just repeating what you already know.

It allows you to practice fluency in your writing, and the articulation of your ideas, using academic power words that you might not be able to use in other places.

Here is an example of the answer with a specific example:

When I consider the definition of self-awareness, I think of what it means to "know oneself." This means knowing what motivates me, and what my strengths and weaknesses are. I know, for example, that I dislike things that waste my time, such as having to explain to students over and over what it is I mean by a specific example. Consequently, rather than continuing to be frustrated by this, I decide it would be better to give students a handout showing them what I mean by a concrete example. This will not only give students an idea of what a specific example looks like, but also give me something to reference in the future just in case somebody missed the explanation I gave in class. In addition, I know from experience that one of the best ways I have learned how to write is by looking at examples, and reverse engineering these examples as a kind of blueprint. By writing a concrete example I am also giving a blueprint for structure and content. Finally, during the process I am able to make self-realizations and gain insights such as just how important self-awareness is to my teaching in general. As a writing instructor, I am constantly asking myself how I would feel receiving an assignment, and what I would learn by doing it so that I don't give assignments that are just "busy work," but have deeper pedagogical objectives. This is a revelation I might not have had without giving a specific example of illustration or if I had just answered with, "I use self-awareness a lot at work."

To recap: the aforementioned example shows you that 1) I understand what self-awareness is, 2) I discover something in writing it, and 3) I improve my powers of articulation and fluency with **academic power words.**

The last thing I would like to say about the importance of specific examples is that it is the quickest way to find out if somebody knows what they are talking about. It's easy for people to talk about some kind of theory or idea, but ask them to provide you with a specific example of illustration and you will quickly see how well they really understand what they are talking about. It is honestly the best litmus test I know to check for understanding. If I ask you what capitalism is, for example, you could say, "an economic system that is based on competition and follows the principles of supply and demand." That sounds great, but what if I asked you to give me a specific example to illustrate how it works. This would quickly separate the wheat from the chaff in terms of who actually understands what this means and who doesn't. In fact, the more expertise somebody has in any given subject, the more easily and abundantly they will be able to give you concrete examples.

Academic Power Words:

The following information is gold.

When my son was in junior high school, he asked me for help on writing an essay, and I told him that he needed to use academic power words in order to help his writing sound more smooth. He didn't know what those were, so I made him a list to keep in front of him as he wrote. He rarely asked me for help after this, and I suspect it is because he figured out the formula. Below you will find a list of academic power words that help make your writing sound professional; make a list of your favorites and tape them to the wall in front of you so that you can refer to them as needed. Once you gain fluency with enough of these words, your formal writing career will become much much easier, not AI easier, but you will need AI less because you will sound like AI. There are too many to use, so find the ones that resonate with you the most, and try to incorporate them as much as possible when you are asked to write something formal like a summary or an analysis. Also, keep in mind that these words are far less effective in poetry and personal essays because they sound too formal for those genres.

To add information:

In addition,
Moreover,
Furthermore,
Also,
Further,
Besides,

To give example:

To illustrate,
To demonstrate,
For instance,
For example,

As an illustration,

To compare:

In the same way,
Similarly,
To explain,
In the same manner,
Likewise,
In a similar fashion,

To contrast:

Nevertheless,
Nonetheless,
But,
However,
Otherwise,
On the contrary,
On the other hand,
In contrast,

To generalize:

To clarify,
In other words,
To explain further,
To clarify.
To rephrase,
Put another way
To paraphrase,

to show result

So,
Therefore,
As a result,
Consequently,
As a consequence,
For this reason,
Thus,

To show time:

Later,
Next,
Following
Meanwhile,
Afterward,
Next,
Then,

To show order:

First,
Second,
Third,
Etc.

Next,
Then,
After that,
Finally,

To emphasize:

Indeed,
Of course,
Certainly,
In fact,
Surely,
Actually,

To summarize:

To summarize,
In summary,
In sum,
In conclusion,
Finally,
To sum up,

Write a sentence using each of the above terms; if you can, try to keep it on a single subject to the best of your ability. The point is to get used to using these terms and how they sound. When writing formally, it is important to get into character and try to sound as academic as possible, even if it sounds forced at first.

In addition to being able to transition elegantly from one paragraph to another, here are some phrases that will help you add quotations with grace and ease:

In a study conducted by ....in (date) it was found that................

In the (text)..................................by........................ he/she/they argue / propose / show / suggest that..

According to......................, a renowned expert in the field / celebrated author / a doctorate in philosophy, etc......................................

According to the............................. statistics show that..

A recent study at.......................................concluded that......................................

How to add more evidence phrases:

In addition, X argues that...

Moreover, there was a study done at.....................................that showed.......................

Furthermore, there is evidence to suggest that..............................

How to introduce counter evidence:

Although ... ... at...................................disagrees and contends that...

Expert X, on the other hand, argues that..

Y disagrees with this assertion, and counters that..................................

Phrases to introduce specific examples:

X writes, for example,..

For example, X writes,..

To illustrate this, X writes...

To make this point clear, X writes..................................

X elucidates this point by saying,..

The basic argument template:

Pick one of the following arguments and use the template below to articulate your position:

Chunky vs. Creamy Peanut Butter

Putting utensils in the dishwasher with the handles down or the handles up

iPhone vs. Samsung

Playstation v. Xbox

In the following essay, I will argue that……………………………………………………………………………………………….because…………………………….. In addition,………………………………………………………….

Although some might argue………………………………….. because……………………………., this doesn't overcome the fact that… … … … … … … … … … … … … … . Moreover,……………………………………………………………… ………………………….

In conclusion, one can see that………………………… because……………………………………….

In the following essay, I will argue that the iPhone 12 is superior to the Samsung Galaxy ultra 22 because the Samsung 22 doesn't allow one to simply text high-quality video to other phones without having to attach it through another application such as Dropbox or Youtube. In addition, there is a greater lag in loading applications on the Galaxy Twelve overall due to some kind of gaming software running in the background, which users cannot turn off.

Although some might argue that the Samsung 22 does allow one to text video, albeit, at a lower quality, this doesn't overcome the fact that this renders the high-quality camera virtually useless. Moreover, it is possible that individuals sending these lower-quality videos might receive ridicule and scorn from other family members using an iPhone which has much higher quality.

In conclusion, one can see that the Galaxy 22 is inferior to the iPhone 12 because of its substandard Android messaging system. In the end, however, I will choose the iPhone because of how well it delivers high-quality videos which are essential to maintaining any kind of clout with one's children.

Here are some more key terms you should know in order to understand writing as a discipline:

Rhetoric: (a fancy way of saying the art of writing) The art of effective or persuasive speaking or writing. It involves techniques and strategies for effectively communicating ideas, influencing an audience, and achieving specific rhetorical goals.

Audience: The intended recipients or readers of a piece of writing or rhetoric. Understanding the audience helps shape the content, tone, and style of the communication.

Considering your audience when writing is extremely important as your tone and writing style will vary greatly whether you're writing a note to a friend or a Ted Talk. I believe this is pretty obvious, but considering the audience is a buzzword right now, I will make sure to talk about it.

What is a **buzzword**? A buzzword is a word or concept that is currently in style in your discipline or field, so you have to adapt to it or look like you are out of date.

Style: The distinctive manner or voice in which a writer or speaker conveys ideas. Style encompasses choices of vocabulary, sentence structure, tone, and rhetorical devices. You might say a person has a very formal writing style, meaning that they sound like a textbook, or you might say they have a very casual style, meaning they speak more colloquially.

Diction: The choice and use of words in writing or speech. Diction influences the tone, style, and overall effectiveness of communication.

Informal diction: We hit the movies after dinner.

Formal diction: We attended the cinema post perfunctory dinner.

Narrative styles and voice:

I want to talk about style, and I have broadly sketched these out into three categories, which I will call, "plain style," "poetic style," and "intellectual style." Of course, these are only my categories and I am sure one could find many more, but I still think it's helpful to look at one scene I have written in three different styles. Then we will talk about the pros and cons of each style.

Trigger warning: I honestly don't have the ability to know what each individual's triggers are, so I will simply ask you to take care of yourself, and if something is triggering to you, you may excuse yourself or not read it. The following examples have marijuana use, so if that is a problem, skip it or plug your ears.

Plain style:

I know plain style sounds boring, but in truth it is one of the most powerful ways to write in my humble opinion. The motive here is to allow the reader to experience what is happening by not telling them very much about what to think or feel or call too much attention to your writing. One simply writes the scene and allows the reader to experience it along with you.

Here is an example:

I ran into this kid Fedina one night in the parking lot of the Safeway, and though I didn't know him well, he rolled down the window of his beat up blue Pinto and asked me if I wanted to get high. I was sixteen at the time, walking home drunk from a friend's house so I figured why not. I got in and saw the floor of his car was strewn with hamburger wrappers and crinkled Coke cans. Fedina's face was full of acne, and his hair was a messy brown nest, as he stuck holes with a pocket knife into one of the Coke cans to turn it into a pipe. He loaded it with some weed then passed it to me and I took a hit. I coughed, and he laughed, then asked me, "Are you taking philosophy with Mr. C?" I said yes, kind of surprised he even knew what philosophy was since I had always thought of him as just another Mt. Vernon stoner.

"Me too," he said, "I love it." I passed him the can, he took a toke, then continued, "I mean have you ever just thought about if there is a God, and like who made the universe."

"Not until Mr. C's class," I said, I said truthfully.

Poetic style:

This is where you write with poetic descriptions so that the reader can experience not only what you are saying, but how you are saying it. You are trying to impress your reader not just with what you are saying, but in how poetically you are saying it. This is what most people think of when they think of "good writing," as it does take some time and practice to be able to render it.

The parking lot at this time of night gleamed like a dark sea as I walked through the parking lot, my breath a thin strip of vapor as I glided toward my car. Then I saw a beat up Pinto sparkling like a blue whale beneath the streetlight, its rusty rib bones laid bare with the passage of time, and inside I saw this kind from school named Fedina at the helm; he rolled down the window as white smoke billowed from the cockpit like a spout, then dissipated into the crisp Winter air. He asked me if I wanted to get high, and I could tell by the sparkling red hue of his eyes that he already was. He was only a senior in high school, but his voice was gruff as an old man's, and reminded me of sandpaper on wood.

Intellectual style:

This is where you tell more than show, and make it more about the ideas and concepts that you want to convery, than the action,

Here is an example:

There is nothing as absurd and awkward as adolescence. That gangly time when one straddles that widening abyss between childhood and adulthood and must wrestle, as Nietzsche, with the diametrically opposed forces of Apollonian order and Dionysian chaos. And so it was during this time, I found myself inside a car with a stranger, smoking marijuana and discussing the very existence of God, right down to the teleological implications of monads. What made this matter even more absurd was that this young man, Fedina, the young tough with whom I was engaging in this rather lofty dialectic, was what in those days we called a "stoner," and not known for his intellectual acumen.   Whereas I had fashioned my identity as more of a pseudo-intellectual or flaneur, who enjoyed a wide range of epistemological modalities from philosophy, TV, and literature, I had only seen Fedina as another member of the lumpenproletariat, as he didn't speak much in class, frequently arrived late, always reeked of coffee and cannabis. But now I was sitting with him in the belly of the whale, and he was asking me whether I believed it was possible to have a free-will given the causal nature of the universe.

I hope that by exaggerating each of these styles about the same scene, you can see the pros and cons of each of them. Of course, no style is set in stone, and you can always use a hybrid of each one, but nonetheless I think it is important to think about your own style, and which you prefer to use and why. This can also be helpful in figuring out what authors you like and why.

In my humble opinion, I like the plain style best most of the time as it allows me to be a co-creator or co-experiencer in the story. It is the classic dictum of "show don't tell."   It is like a scene in the movie without a voiceover.

I do, however, also appreciate a well wrought poetic description, and don't mind poetic writing, especially when it is a hybrid with the plain style. By this I mean telling the story in a straightforward manner, with a flourish of lyrical brilliance once in a while. I am personally not a huge fan of poetic writing that goes on and on without much happening by way of narrative, but that doesn't mean you can't love that kind of writing.

Intellectual style is all about thinking of your audience. Oftentimes it can be alienating to use an intellectual style if your readership isn't intellectual. If you are going to make a reference to ancient Greek literature, do you expect your reader to know it? Or do you need to introduce it so that everyone, even if they haven't studied Greek literature, can get on board like Ulyssses. I personally don't write in this style very much, but I did get a kick out of it this time, using it to write about two stoners in a Safeway parking lot. The truth is that when I was in college, I thought the intellectual style of writing was the only kind of "good writing." I thought I had to use as many big words as possible to sound smart, and it wasn't until years later that I saw the power of writing in a more plain style, and allowing the scenes to speak for themselves.

In the end, of course, these styles can be applied to narrative and expository modes of writing, and it is up to you which you would like to employ. As a beginner, I would recommend the plain style, but as you progress you might want to play with other styles or hybrids (no pun intended). I have loved authors in all different styles and hybrids thereof, and in any case, I hope this has helped you to think more about style in writing, and audience.

More key terms to understand the discipline of writing:

Purpose: The specific goal or intention behind a piece of writing or rhetoric. The purpose can vary, such as to inform, persuade, entertain, make somebody laugh or provoke a riot.

Thesis statement: A concise and focused statement that presents the main argument or claim in an essay or speech. It provides direction and structure to the overall piece.

Topic sentence: the sentence at the start of a paragraph that lets the reader know what the paragraph is going to be about.

Can you identify the topic sentences in the expository paragraphs we looked at earlier? What are they?

Evidence: Facts, examples, statistics, or other supporting material used to bolster and validate an argument or claim. Evidence strengthens the credibility and persuasiveness of a piece of writing.

Once you make an argument, whatever it is, the next thing a person is going to want is evidence.

Do any of the above expository paragraphs have any evidence to back their claims?

Claim: In the context of writing, a claim refers to a statement or proposition that asserts a specific position or viewpoint on a particular topic. It is the central argument or thesis.

Persuasion: The act of influencing or convincing others to adopt a particular viewpoint or take specific action. Persuasive writing often employs rhetorical techniques to appeal to emotions, logic, and credibility.

Structure: The organization and arrangement of ideas within a piece of writing or rhetoric. It includes elements such as introduction, body paragraphs, transitions, and conclusion.

Ethos, Pathos, and Logos: These are the three rhetorical appeals used to persuade an audience. Ethos appeals to credibility and trustworthiness, pathos appeals to emotions, and logos appeals to logic and reason.

Which one of these appeals to ethos, pathos, and logos.

You should recycle because natural resources are finite and soon we will run out of them.

I've got a PHD in recycling, and a masters in Green Studies at Environmental University.

Recycle or we will all die horrible deaths!

Genre: A category or type of writing characterized by its form, content, and intended purpose. Examples of genres include essays, speeches, narratives, poems, and argumentative texts.

Cohesion: The quality of a piece of writing that ensures its parts are logically connected and flow smoothly. Cohesion is achieved through effective use of transitional words and phrases, sentence structure, and logical sequencing of ideas.

Context: The circumstances, background, or environment in which a piece of writing or rhetoric is situated. Understanding the context helps interpret and analyze the message more accurately.

Plagiarism: The act of using someone else's words, ideas, or work without proper attribution or acknowledgment. This includes the use of artificial intelligence without properly citing the work. Plagiarism is considered unethical and can have serious consequences.

Visual rhetoric: The use of visual elements, such as images, graphs, charts, or layout, to enhance the persuasive power or appeal of a piece of communication. Visual rhetoric is commonly employed in advertisements, memes, infographics, and presentations.

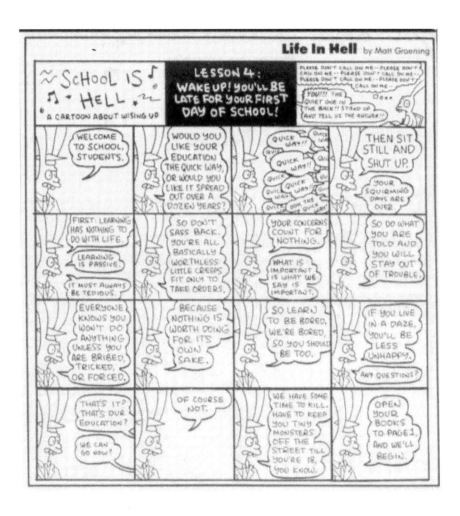

How to write a **personal narrative:**

A Basic Overview of How to Write Narratives:

Introduction to the *deluxe scene:*

First of all let me say that there is no "right" way to write, and that everyone is going to develop their own unique voice and style, but in the meantime I want to give you some concepts that will help you write personal narratives regardless of your style. I have read many books, and studied many years to be able to distill these concepts to you in an easily digestible way. The first concept I want to talk about is what I call the "deluxe scene." The purpose of a deluxe scene is to create a movie in the reader's mind so that they feel like they are taking part in your world.

Below is an example that I will later break down for you into parts to show how it works. The techniques here can be used for fiction or creative nonfiction stories:

Deluxe Scene:

The bar was tiny, right beside a river where you could see boats bobbing on the water. On the wall hung old black and white pictures of old celebrities who had been there, (Carrot Top, Vanilla ice). There was even an old DEVO hat on top of a rusted beer keg, signed by somebody in the band. My blind date walked in late, wearing a big orange sweatshirt with rainbows on the sleeve. Her blonde hair was frazzled, and she wasn't wearing any make up. There was a tattoo of a unicorn on her neck that seemed oddly fitting, as she spied me, then made her way toward me, bumping into everyone as she made her way to the back. "Hey," she said, "You must be Max. I am sorry I am late, but my brother wouldn't give me the keys to his car because he said he needed it to go see his dealer."

"No problem," I said, shaking her hand. I wasn't sure if she was kidding, so I let this information slide, but kept it in the back of my mind as a potential red flag. I had already dated too many addicts to want to go down that road again. Lizzy had been recommended to me by a friend of mine whose point of view I very much admired and trusted. "You've got to meet Lizzy," she said, "She is a wonderful nut job."

Now, normally most people would balk at the term "nut job" but to me it was code for interesting in this small town just outside of L.A. where most of the real "nut jobs" had moved to. But not Lizzy. The first thing she says after noticing all the stars on the wall is, "Christ, I hate celebrities!" So at least we have this in common, for now.

End of scene.

Hopefully, this story pulled you in as a reader by painting a clear and concise scene. Sometimes in writing you hear the idea that "showing" is better than "telling," and though I believe there is a time and place for both, a deluxe scene is all about showing.

To continue the story I would just tell the reader what happened next or move through time with a transition that would sound something like this:

I didn't see Lizzie again for a few weeks then she called to ask me if I wanted to go bowling.

Or these:

We saw each other a few times before we had our first fight.

This is the basic formula for writing a narrative scene + summary/exposition/time change.

So, now let's break down this deluxe scene down into parts:

First of all, it is a scene, and a scene is something that takes place at one time and place. It isn't a description of something that goes on for months or years.

You can summarize time, but it's no longer a scene. It's called a *scene summary*, and it would sound something like this.

We went to that same bar for months, talking about everything and nothing. We played pool. We held hands. We smoked cigarettes, and watched ball games. She wasn't a fan of football, and neither was I, but we placed penny bets on ridiculous things like what quarter would there be the first interception, and how many times the ball would be fumbled.

After this, I would then go back to another scene to show the next important moment or "beat," as it is sometimes called, in the relationship.

Now, back to the deluxe scene. It should also give a description of the place with two concrete visual details.

A concrete visual detail isn't just saying "a bar" or "classroom" or "a man" but something more detailed, such as "a bar with bamboo festooned with lights" and "a classroom with crumbling blue paint," and "a man with a grizzled beard, hunched over like a broken bush." Of course, you don't have to use concrete visual details, but I hope you can see how powerful they can be to help your reader imagine the story happening.

In addition to a description of place, a deluxe scene should also have a description of character, again with at least two concrete visuals, such as "grizzled beard," or "unicorn tattoo."

Of course, if you are writing about more than one character in a scene, this could get cumbersome, so for now let's stick to one other character in a scene with you.

Next there should be some dialogue. **Dialogue** means we get to hear the other character speak, and you respond in some way.

And finally, last but not least, the key to a good narrative is what I like to call the **inner response.** The inner response is where you tell the reader how you are thinking and feeling as things are happening. Without it, the reader doesn't know why they should care, or what is at stake for the speaker.

An example of inner response from my deluxe scene above:

"Now, normally most people would balk at the term "nut job" but to me it was code for interesting in this little town…"

This inner response shows you what the character is thinking and feeling, and reveals more of who they are.

So to summarize the key parts of a deluxe scene:

Description of place with **two concrete visual details**

Description of **character** with two concrete visuals, and an introduction if needed.

Dialogue

Inner Response

Introductions in personal essay writing:

An introduction is another element that may come into play, especially if you are writing a shorter story. Since we don't have much time to develop characters in shorter work, it is important to establish relationships right away with what I like to call introductions. This allows the reader to quickly understand who other characters are in relationship to the narrator.
In the scene above, for example, the intro is very short since it is a blind date, and the speaker doesn't know much about her, but other stories may have characters who are more intimate to the narrator. In addition, you could be writing about a place or something that nobody knows much about, so it would also require a quick introduction. Here are some examples of what good introductions sound like for people, places, and things. An intro to a person: This could either be just the physical description if it's a stranger or a quick summary of the relationship if it is somebody the narrator knows.

Let's say I was writing a story about my uncle Jim, I might introduce him like this.

My uncle Jim had been in and out of my life since I was a kid, always making me laugh with his absurdist humor, like the time he made us sing a song about hot dogs for a half-hour on a camping trip. My mother thought it was odd, but it was the only thing I remember from that trip.

Continue on with the story..

Suddenly we smelled smoke, and the fire alarm went off…etc.

Introductions to Places:

Sometimes you need to introduce a place to your reader, if it is not something common knowledge or if you want to explore a common place in more detail.

Paris was a city like no other I'd been to. There were old European buildings, traffic, pollution, but everywhere you looked there were pockets of beauty, golden statues, glass pyramids, and, of course, the Eiffel Tower that rose into the sky like the stem of a black rose.

Introductions to Things:

Sometimes you need to introduce an activity or object that the reader may not be familiar with, such as bullfighting or a vape pen. Now, of course, some audiences might be familiar with bullfighting or vape pens, but as a rule bullfighting is still rare, and a vape pen is still new enough that many readers might not be familiar with them, so it's up to you to figure out whether or not they need introductions. In my view, they never hurt, and sometimes yield interesting discoveries in writing about them as if your reader isn't familiar.

I call this a deluxe scene because it really does paint a picture in the reader's mind, and it yields novel quality writing, but in writing personal essays, you might want to pare down the scene so that it's still specific but perhaps not as detailed, because you have less time to make your points. Unless otherwise specified, most of your narrative paragraphs should be pared down like this:

Blind dates can often be awkward, and generally don't end up well, but that wasn't the case with a young man I met once named Lizzy. She had frizzy blond hair and blue eyes, and we met at a dive bar in California. I immediately thought she was funny and interesting. She made dead-pan jokes that I couldn't tell if she was serious or not, like telling me her brother was a drug dealer when, in fact, he was an accountant in Fresno. When she first told me this, there was a moment I was worried she was a drug addict herself due to my long history of dating addicts of one kind or another, but she was, for the most part, a "normie." The exception to this was her relationship to scratch-off tickets, which I will get into later. For the most part, however, Lizzy and I hit it off very well and soon we were doing a lot of things together like hiking, biking, and going for trips to LA, a city we both had a love-hate relationship with.

Even though the above is a basic narrative, it still has the basics of taking place in a specific time and place, some description, dialogue and inner response.

Punctuation for dialogue:

Here is a basic refresher on how to punctuate dialogue in a narrative:

Once upon a time there lived a Prince, and his name was Hank. He enjoyed gambling, and pizza. One day he saw his friend the frog and said, "Hello Frog."
Introduce a quote with a comma, and put the period (and all other ending punctuation marks) inside the quotation marks, not outside of them. Do not write, for example, "Hello Frog".

Just look at how terrible that period looks outside the quotation marks, unless you are from England, etc.

Once upon a time there lived a Prince, and his name was Hank. He enjoyed gambling, and pizza. One day he saw his friend the frog and said, "Hello Frog."
"Hello Prince," said the Frog.

Indent a paragraph tab or five spaces to show there is a new speaker, in this case Frog. Don't put a period after "Hello Prince" when there is a tagline like "he said," or "she said." Put a comma there, until the end of the tag line. You write: "Hello Prince," said the Frog." You do not write: "Hello Prince." Said the Frog.

Once upon a time there lived a Prince, and his name was Hank. He enjoyed gambling, and pizza. One day he saw his friend the frog and said, "Hello Frog."
"Hello Prince," said the Frog.
"You look green today," said the Prince, laughing.
"I am a damn Frog."
"Oh, you're right," said the Prince, adjusting his crown. "Don't get pissy"
With that, the Frog jumped away.

The End

Notice on the third line of dialogue, I didn't even have to use the tagline, "said the Frog" anymore. That is because I already know who is speaking by the paragraph indentation. The speaking order has been established. Look also at the fancy way I divided up the dialogue with some action in the fourth line of dialogue. You can do that too.

For text message dialogue, I would use the old colon as below:

Fred texted me: "Hello."

"Hello," I texted back.

Fred: R we going for pizza lol.

Me: Yes (pizza emoji)

Fred: (thumb up emoji)

From what I can tell from researching how to punctuate social media, the rules on how to do this are still being sorted out, so this will do for now (Lol, heart emoji, crying face).

In class assignment: write a short paired-down scene with dialogue.

Some examples of why punctuation is important:

Sure, here are some humorous examples of how punctuation can significantly change the meaning of a sentence:

Without punctuation: "Let's eat grandpa."
With punctuation: "Let's eat, grandpa."
The punctuation changes this from a rather gruesome statement into a gentle invitation to dinner!

Without punctuation: "I enjoy cooking my family and my pets."
With punctuation: "I enjoy cooking, my family, and my pets."
Here, the commas drastically alter the meaning of the sentence, making the speaker's interests clear rather than suggesting some worrying habits!

Without punctuation: "She found a cooking pot large."
With punctuation: "She found a cooking pot, large."
This punctuation change modifies the meaning from a nonsensical sentence to a simple description of a large pot.

Without punctuation: "A woman without her man is nothing."
With punctuation: "A woman: without her, man is nothing."
This clever play with punctuation drastically shifts the sentence's emphasis and meaning.

Without punctuation: "I love my friends dogs and kids."
With punctuation: "I love my friends, dogs, and kids."
Commas turn this from a potentially confusing statement into a simple list of affection!

Without punctuation: "The panda eats shoots and leaves."
With punctuation: "The panda eats, shoots, and leaves."
This example is a classic that demonstrates the vital role of commas. In the second sentence, the panda appears to have developed some alarmingly aggressive behaviors!

Without punctuation: "Don't stop eating people."
With punctuation: "Don't stop eating, people."
The first statement is rather sinister, while the corrected one with punctuation is simply urging people to continue eating.

Without punctuation: "Can we eat mom."
With punctuation: "Can we eat, mom?"
A simple comma and a question mark transform this from a frightening proposition to an innocent question at dinnertime.

Some notes on getting beyond black and white / dichotomous thinking:

After reading the essay "On Black and White Thinking," it is important also to look at some of the most common barriers you will encounter when trying to engage in a more dialectical manner, as well as some strategies to overcome them.

Barriers to authentic dialogue:

Emotions
Emotional issues
Triggers
Chemicals / Addiction
Hangry
Personalities
Ego
Identity

Fear of the unknown
Fear of being weak / wrong
Lack of trust
Negative self-talk
Unproductive frames
Superficial frames

Strategies for overcoming dichotomous thinking:

Take a time out to cool down
Change the frame to a productive/ dialectical one
Change the frame to real the emotional issue: why are you angry?
Talk explicitly about the argument itself and where it is leading: What is the motive of it? Venting, problem solving, etc.
Is there anything that can be said to change the person's mind or is it about something else?
Does an apology help? If not, why not?
Use active listening / Hold space
Have boundaries
Own what is yours if you have made a mistake, apologize
Recognize when you are "in an issue" or if the person you are talking with is "in an issue."

Having an issue is a vast and complex topic, but it usually means when the emotion doesn't fit the crime, so a deeper issue is at work. For example, I get enraged by somebody forgetting to take out the garbage, because my alcoholic father never did and so I am in a childhood issue about my father, and it's not about the garbage per se. Again, this is what therapists do, but having a basic understanding can be helpful.

Try to switch from absolute statements to qualified ones. You never take out the garbage. You always forget my birthday. Vs.

You seldom take out the garbage, and you forgot my birthday twice.

See if you can repeat the other person's argument without sarcasm and vice versa.

Recognize when somebody isn't in a place to listen.

Don't try to teach a pig to whistle; it wastes your time, and annoys the pig.

Recognize this is hard for everybody, and be compassionate with yourself and others.

Drink Water
Drink coffee
Talk with a friend
Eat
Get a counselor
Exercise
Meditate
Climb a mountain
See social media and self-help culture for more examples.

Notes, words, concepts, epipahnies and connections:

Chapter 2: Intelligences, Motivation, and Mental Health

The following is an excerpt from Mark Manson, the author of the book "The Subtle Art of Not Giving a F&*^%":

For most of my adolescence and young adulthood, I fantasized about being a musician—a rock star, in particular. Any badass guitar song I heard, I would always close my eyes and envision myself up onstage playing it to the screams of the crowd, people absolutely losing their minds to my sweet finger-noodling.

This fantasy could keep me occupied for hours on end. The fantasizing continued through college, even after I dropped out of music school and stopped playing seriously.

But even then it was never a question of if I'd ever be up playing in front of screaming crowds, but when. I was biding my time before I could invest the proper amount of time and effort into getting out there and making it work. First, I needed to finish school. Then, I needed to make money. Then, I needed to find the time. Then… nothing.

Despite fantasizing about this for over half of my life, the reality never came. And it took me a long time and a lot of negative experiences to finally figure out why: I didn't actually want it.

I was in love with the result—the image of me onstage, people cheering, me rocking out, pouring my heart into what I'm playing—but I wasn't in love with the process. And because of that, I failed at it. Repeatedly. Hell, I didn't even try hard enough to fail at it. I hardly tried at all.

The daily drudgery of practicing, the logistics of finding a group and rehearsing, the pain of finding gigs and actually getting people to show up and give a shit. The broken strings, the blown tube amp, hauling 40 pounds of gear to and from rehearsals with no car.

It's a mountain of a dream and a mile-high climb to the top. And what took me a long time to discover was that I didn't like to climb much. I just liked to imagine the top.

Our culture would tell me that I've somehow failed myself, that I'm a quitter or a loser. Self-help would say that I either wasn't courageous enough, determined enough or I didn't believe in myself enough.[6] The entrepreneurial/start-up crowd would tell me that I chickened out on my dream and gave in to my conventional social conditioning.[7] I'd be told to do affirmations[8] or join a mastermind group or manifest, or something.

But the truth is far less interesting than that: I thought I wanted something, but it turns out I didn't. End of story.

I wanted the reward and not the struggle. I wanted the result and not the process. I was in love not with the fight, but only the victory.

And life doesn't work that way.

Who you are is defined by the values you are willing to struggle for. People who enjoy the struggles of a gym are the ones who get in good shape.[9] People who enjoy long work weeks and the politics of the corporate ladder are the ones who move up it.[10] People who enjoy the stresses and uncertainty of the starving artist life are ultimately the ones who live it and make it.[11]

This is not a call for willpower or "grit."12 This is not another admonition of "no pain, no gain."13

This is the most simple and basic component of life: our struggles determine our successes. So, friend, choose your struggles wisely.

This article is an updated excerpt from my book, The Subtle Art of Not Giving a F&*^: A Counterintuitive Guide to Living A Good Life

End of excerpt.

I really like this idea in conjunction with multiple intelligence theory, and Emotional Intelligence theory because of its simple truth. No matter what you end up doing in life, it will involve problem solving of some kind, so it is important to find problems that you enjoy solving. As an educator, my problem is getting students to be better writers and critical thinkers, and I happen to love that problem. If I were a boxer, my problem would be knocking my opponent out with the right combination of punches, and though I enjoy watching boxing, I do not love getting hit, so this was not the profession for me.

Trivial fact: boxing is known also as the sweet science.

Multiple intelligences:

Read the article on multiple intelligence theory by Howard Gardner and know what the following terms mean:

Multiple Intelligence Theory: Multiple Intelligence Theory is a psychological framework developed by Howard Gardner that suggests individuals possess different types of intelligences, each representing a unique way of processing and understanding information.

Intelligence: *In the context of Multiple Intelligence Theory, intelligence refers to the ability to understand, learn, and apply knowledge effectively.* According to Gardner, intelligence goes beyond traditional measures (such as IQ) and encompasses a range of cognitive abilities.

Linguistic Intelligence: Linguistic intelligence refers to the ability to use language effectively, including reading, writing, speaking, and listening. Individuals with linguistic intelligence often excel in activities such as storytelling, debating, or writing poetry.

Logical-Mathematical Intelligence: Logical-mathematical intelligence refers to the capacity to reason logically, think analytically, and solve complex mathematical or logical problems. Individuals with this intelligence tend to excel in fields such as mathematics, computer programming, or scientific research.

Spatial Intelligence: Spatial intelligence refers to the ability to visualize and manipulate objects in space, perceive patterns, and navigate the physical world effectively. Individuals with spatial intelligence may have a talent for architecture, visual arts, or map reading.

Musical Intelligence: Musical intelligence involves sensitivity to sounds, rhythm, pitch, and melody. People with musical intelligence often exhibit talents in playing instruments, composing music, or recognizing patterns in auditory stimuli.

Bodily-Kinesthetic Intelligence: Bodily-kinesthetic intelligence relates to the ability to control one's body movements, manipulate objects skillfully, and excel in physical activities. Athletes, dancers, and surgeons often demonstrate high bodily-kinesthetic intelligence.

Interpersonal Intelligence: Interpersonal intelligence refers to the capacity to understand and interact effectively with others, showing empathy, social skills, and emotional intelligence. Individuals with strong interpersonal intelligence are often natural leaders, mediators, or counselors.

Intrapersonal Intelligence: Intrapersonal intelligence involves self-reflection, self-awareness, and a deep understanding of one's own emotions, strengths, and weaknesses. People with intrapersonal intelligence tend to be self-motivated, introspective, and capable of pursuing personal goals.

Naturalistic Intelligence: Naturalistic intelligence involves a heightened sensitivity and understanding of the natural world, including plants, animals, and natural phenomena. Individuals with naturalistic intelligence may excel in areas such as ecology, botany, or environmental science.

When I first read Howard Gardner, the aforementioned intelligences were the only ones he talked about, but in subsequent years, he added the following, which I think are very interesting. You aren't expected to know them, but I think they are inherently interesting:

Existential Intelligence: Existential intelligence refers to the ability to contemplate deep philosophical and existential questions, such as the meaning of life, the nature of existence, and the human condition. Individuals with strong existential intelligence may be drawn to philosophy, theology, or contemplative practices.

Emotional Intelligence: Emotional intelligence involves the ability to perceive, understand, and manage one's own emotions, as well as recognize and empathize with the emotions of others. It plays a crucial role in interpersonal relationships, leadership, and overall well-being.

Cultural Intelligence: Cultural intelligence refers to the capacity to interact effectively and adapt to diverse cultural contexts. It involves understanding and respecting different cultural norms, values, and behaviors, and being able to navigate cultural differences with sensitivity.

Technological Intelligence: Technological intelligence refers to the ability to understand and utilize technology effectively. It involves being adept at using digital tools, troubleshooting technical issues, and keeping up with the rapidly evolving technological landscape.

Creative Intelligence: Creative intelligence encompasses the ability to generate original ideas, think outside the box, and approach problems in innovative ways. It involves a combination of imagination, divergent thinking, and the willingness to take risks.

Analytical Intelligence: Analytical intelligence involves the capacity to analyze complex information, identify patterns, and make logical connections. It plays a crucial role in critical thinking, problem-solving, and decision-making.

Practical Intelligence: Practical intelligence, also known as "street smarts," refers to the ability to apply knowledge and skills effectively in real-life situations. It involves adaptability, common sense, and the capacity to navigate practical challenges.

Intuitive Intelligence: Intuitive intelligence involves the ability to make quick and accurate decisions based on instinct or gut feelings. It taps into subconscious knowledge and allows individuals to rely on their intuition in uncertain or ambiguous situations.

Collaborative Intelligence: Collaborative intelligence refers to the ability to work effectively in teams, foster cooperation, and leverage the strengths of others to achieve common goals. It involves communication skills, empathy, and the capacity to build positive relationships.

Emotional Intelligence:

In the seminal work "Emotional Intelligence: Why It Can Matter More Than IQ," Daniel Goleman challenges conventional wisdom surrounding the assessment of human intelligence and aptitude. Published in 1995, this influential book presents a multifaceted view of intelligence, one that includes emotional competencies and awareness.

Goleman introduces the concept of emotional intelligence (EI) as encompassing five key domains: self-awareness, self-regulation, motivation, empathy, and social skills. Unlike traditional intelligence metrics, such as IQ, which assess cognitive abilities, emotional intelligence emphasizes an individual's capacity to recognize, understand, and manage their emotions, as well as to empathize with others (Goleman, 1995).

Throughout the book, Goleman explores the application of emotional intelligence across various life spheres, including personal relationships, professional environments, parenting, and self-development. He asserts that EI is often a superior predictor of success in these domains compared to conventional intelligence measures.

An essential aspect of Goleman's argument is the integration of emotional intelligence within the educational system. He posits that cultivating emotional competencies within schools can yield more compassionate, responsible, and socially adept individuals, thereby contributing positively to societal well-being.

Furthermore, Goleman delves into the neuroscientific underpinnings of emotional intelligence. By exploring how the brain processes emotions, he bridges the gap between theoretical constructs and biological foundations, enhancing the credibility of his arguments.

A critical element of "Emotional Intelligence" is the author's critique of the overreliance on traditional intelligence measures like IQ. Goleman argues that such measures present an incomplete and narrow view of human potential, neglecting vital emotional aspects that are equally significant for human functioning.

In conclusion, Goleman's "Emotional Intelligence" presents a paradigm shift in understanding human intelligence and potential. By emphasizing the importance of emotional competencies, the book has had a profound impact on various fields, from psychology to business. Despite some critiques regarding the clarity and measurement of the concept, the idea of emotional intelligence has resonated widely, underscoring the importance of emotions in our daily lives and encouraging a more holistic approach to personal development and success (Open AI).

Read the article on Emotional Intelligence by Daniel Goleman, and know what the following terms mean:

Key Terms you should know:

Emotional intelligence, often abbreviated as EQ (Emotional Quotient), refers to the ability to understand, manage, and effectively express one's own feelings, as well as engage and navigate successfully with the emotions of others. It involves skills such as emotional awareness, the ability to apply emotions to tasks like problem-solving, and the capacity to manage emotions, which includes both regulating one's own emotions and cheering up or calming down other people. The importance of emotional intelligence lies in its profound impact on personal and professional life. High EQ is linked to success in many areas, including relationship building, leadership, team performance, and decision-making. It provides the foundation for empathy and effective interpersonal interactions, and plays a crucial role in enhancing one's mental well-being, resilience, and overall life satisfaction.

Self-Awareness: Self-awareness is the ability to recognize and understand one's own emotions, strengths, weaknesses, and values. It involves being in tune with one's thoughts, feelings, and behaviors.

Self-Regulation: Self-regulation is the skill of managing and controlling one's emotions, impulses, and reactions in different situations. It involves maintaining emotional balance, controlling anger or frustration, and adapting to changing circumstances.

Empathy: Empathy is the capacity to understand and share the emotions and perspectives of others. It involves being sensitive to others' feelings, demonstrating compassion, and being able to see situations from their point of view.

Social Skills: Social skills encompass the ability to build and maintain positive relationships, communicate effectively, and navigate social interactions. It involves active listening, verbal and nonverbal communication, conflict resolution, and cooperation.

Emotional Awareness: Emotional awareness refers to the ability to identify and recognize one's own emotions accurately. It involves understanding the nuances of different emotions and being able to label and differentiate them.

Emotional Regulation: Emotional regulation is the skill of managing and modulating one's own emotions. It involves being able to control emotional responses, handle stress, and adapt to changing situations without being overwhelmed by emotions.

Empathetic Listening: Empathetic listening is the practice of actively listening to others with genuine interest and empathy. It involves giving full attention, understanding the speaker's emotions, and responding in a supportive and compassionate manner.

Motivation: Motivation in the context of emotional intelligence refers to the ability to harness and direct emotions to drive goal-oriented behavior. It involves being self-motivated, resilient in the face of setbacks, and maintaining a positive attitude.

Relationship Management: Relationship management is the skill of building and maintaining healthy and productive relationships with others. It involves effective communication, conflict resolution, teamwork, and the ability to inspire and influence others positively.

Key questions about multiple intelligence theory:

How can being aware of this concept and how it applies to you be helpful to you in your daily life?

Are there kinds of intelligences you have observed in yourself and others that can't be put into one of Gardner's categories?

Do you think intelligence should be strictly defined as IQ? Why or why not?

Would it be possible to test for multiple intelligences? How?

A comment on emotional intelligence:

Most of the articles about Emotional Intelligence are framed around the idea of how this intelligence can help you in the workplace, but just as importantly, this intelligence can help you foster better relationships in life. In my opinion, these skills should be at the forefront of every curriculum, but they are also difficult to deal with. Of course, everyone comes from different backgrounds with different levels of trauma, neurodivergence, and biological factors that can also affect one's EI, so it is important not to judge ourselves or others on where we are on this journey. Moreover, if you are struggling with any mental health issues, here is the number for the Counseling Department at Lane Community College, as well as where it is located: In-person Counseling - Call

541-463-3600 to schedule or come to the Counseling Center Building 1, room 103.

Artificial Intelligence:

Before we delve deeper into the promise and perils of Artificial Intelligence, I want to give an overview of my beliefs about Large Language Models, such as Chat GPT, Bard, etc. especially in regard to how it can and should be used in my class, starting with some good quotes/

"Everything has been thought of before, but the problem is to think of it again."

–Johann Wolfgang von Goethe

"Forget artificial intelligence – in the brave new world of big data, it's artificial idiocy we should be looking out for."

—Tom Chatfield

"Before we work on artificial intelligence why don't we do something about natural stupidity?"

—Steve Polyak

Some General Notes on Chat GPT and AI in general:

The easiest way to think about open AI to avoid complications is to think of it as a new and improved internet that is faster, more efficient, and intelligent, but just as it wouldn't be a good idea to copy and paste something from the internet and claim it as your own work, neither is it a good idea to do that with AI. AI basically gets all of its content by plagiarizing the work of humans, so treat its writing as you would another person's paper. Give credit where credit is due. You can simply write:

According to Open AI, "75 percent of college students are now using AI in some capacity."

Or

The use of AI is on the rise: "75 percent of college students are now using AI in some capacity" (Open AI).

If you find a specific source within Open AI, you can just write:

According to an expert cited by Open AI from the New York Times, "Your job won't be replaced by AI, but by somebody using AI."

Or

"Your job won't be replaced by AI, but by somebody using AI," (Open AI/New York Times)

In addition, you can use the sources AI gives, but be careful to cross-reference them with the primary source documents to make sure they are legitimate sources of information. Like Wikipedia before it, AI is a good starting place for research and information, but AI has been known to be wrong and to "hallucinate," which means giving answers that sound legitimate but are literal BS.

Open AI, however, is very good at giving outlines and rough drafts of papers, but the problem is that you will be so tempted to use it that you will either end up plagiarizing or you will spend just a much time turning it into your own thing and it will sound probably sound awkward when it is finished.

The purpose of writing isn't just about the writing per se, but honing your ability to articulate yourself in more complex ways. It's about increasing your ability to synthesize, summarize, process, and analyze complex ideas, and the more you have AI do this for you, the less you will gain in terms of language fluency. You will remain stagnant at the level where you started letting AI do the thinking for you. Moreover, it could become a habit that is hard to break, which could cost you down the line. I pride myself on being an independent thinker, but still find myself tempted to go straight to AI for some things I should try to figure out on my own first.

The capacity to articulate oneself in language might not matter as much if you are working at lower skills jobs, but the higher you go up the ladder of skill and commensurate pay, it usually becomes more important that you can demonstrate your competence to articulate and solve problems. In my interview for my position here at Lane, for example, I had to articulate my vision for teaching in a way that I wouldn't have been able to, had I not spent weeks honing my cover letter and resume, figuring out for myself how I was qualified. If I had had Chat GPT do that work, I believe I would have been much less confident in what I was talking about, even if my cover letter sounded good. Without the work I put in, my lack of skill would be glaring, and I am sure I would not have been hired.

That is why I would also highly recommend that whenever you are given a challenging intellectual task to complete, such as an analysis of a text, I suggest you try to figure out the answer on your own before consulting AI or the internet in general.   The reason is that you will be denying yourself the mental challenge and dare I say "joy" that comes with discovering something on your own. In addition, you are likely to accept whatever the AI (internet) says, instead of your own idea which may be just as valid. In other words, relying completely on AI for your thinking won't help you gain the intellectual confidence you need in order to succeed.

The temptation is great, I get it. We are busy, overwhelmed, and the idea of having a robot do our homework for us sounds like a dream come true, but imagine your are paying money to take a Karate class, but somebody offers you a Karate Robot that will take it for you, so you send it in your place, so you can have more free time. That sounds absurd, right? But that's exactly what you do when you have a robot take any class for you. You are paying to learn new skills, and knowledge.

The problem comes when you have to defend yourself without your robot on the street or in a job interview to be a karate instructor. They ask you to show your stuff, and you got nothing.

In conclusion, AI is here to stay. It is a powerful tool with mind-blowing capabilities, for sure, but it has problems. It has bias according to how it was programmed, and just like Google that originally looked like an unbiased search engine at the start, soon became biased toward ad revenue; the same is probably already happening with AI. In addition, AI makes mistakes all the time, and if you don't already know what you are talking about, it can really undermine your work. Like most things, the more competent you are, the better you will be able to use this tool. I have decent mastery over certain works of literature, for example, so I know when a chatbot is full of it, but if I were to ask it questions in a domain I wasn't familiar with, I would have to cross-reference it to make sure it wasn't hallucinating on me. Finally, AI is excellent with overviews and main ideas, but it is still quite weak at specificity. It is also quite dull sounding most of the time. When I read your papers, I am not looking for robotic perfection with grammar, but signs that you are struggling to articulate challenging ideas. Grammar and punctuation to me are all in service of getting your point across, so even if you write something that might be verbally clunky, as long as I understand clearly what you are saying, I don't mind it. It's part of your voice, part of where you are at in your learning journey.

Honestly, the takeaway I have from reflecting on this is that AI is the calculator for language. It can do all the work for you in much less time than you can by yourself, but that doesn't take away your need to know how to think, problem-solve, and articulate yourself. In the end, it is those skills that will determine where you end up in life, and how happy you are with the results.

Key terms for AI:

Cross-referencing: checking sources outside of the AI ecosystem.

Filter Bias: the bias of AI results that come with the parameters set up by the programmers, whatever they may be

Hallucinations: When AI spits out an answer that sounds convincing, but is completely made up, and does not correspond with reality

Plagiarism: trying to pass of somebody's else work (including a robot's) as if it were your own

(grammar and spelling checkers are excluded)

Here is what CHAT GPT said when I asked it: What are some dangers of students using CHAT GPT for composition classes:

While ChatGPT can be a valuable tool for college students, there are potential dangers associated with relying too heavily on it in composition classes. Here are some considerations:

Plagiarism: Students may be tempted to use ChatGPT to generate entire essays or sections of their assignments without fully understanding the content. This can lead to unintentional plagiarism if they fail to properly attribute the generated text or if they present it as their original work.

Lack of critical thinking: Relying solely on ChatGPT for composition assignments may hinder the development of critical thinking and analytical skills. Students need to engage actively with the writing process, which involves brainstorming, researching, organizing ideas, and evaluating sources. Overdependence on ChatGPT may limit their ability to think independently and generate unique insights.

Inaccurate or biased information: ChatGPT is trained on a vast amount of data, including online sources, which can contain inaccurate or biased information. Students should be cautious when incorporating information generated by ChatGPT without verifying it through reliable and credible sources.

Limited improvement of writing skills: Writing is a skill that improves through practice, feedback, and revision. Relying too heavily on ChatGPT may prevent students from honing their own writing abilities and identifying areas for improvement. It's important for students to actively engage in the writing process and seek feedback from instructors and peers.

To mitigate these dangers, instructors should clearly communicate expectations regarding the use of AI language models, provide guidance on responsible usage, and encourage students to develop their critical thinking and writing skills through other means, such as class discussions, workshops, and writing exercises. Balancing the use of AI tools with traditional writing practices can help students maximize the benefits while minimizing the potential risks. (AI)

Although these are pretty much the same key issues I brought up, there is one thing that the robot did not address in its concerns that I did. It said nothing about how using AI can rob you of the "joy" that comes from figuring out something on your own, and maybe that is because the joy of learning is a uniquely human thing that AI doesn't understand. Yet?!

Read the article on AI, and know what the following terms mean:

Artificial Intelligence (AI): Artificial Intelligence refers to the development of computer systems that can perform tasks that typically require human intelligence. It involves the simulation of human cognitive functions such as learning, problem-solving, and decision-making.

An algorithm typically takes input data, processes it through a series of operations, and produces an output, which is the desired result or solution to the problem at hand.

Probabilistic Outcome: A probabilistic outcome refers to a result or event that is determined by chance or uncertainty and is described in terms of probabilities. In contrast to deterministic outcomes, where the result is entirely predictable given the initial conditions and rules, probabilistic outcomes involve an element of randomness.

Large Language Models: Large Language Models (LLMs) are AI systems designed to understand and generate human language. They leverage large datasets to learn patterns, grammar, and context to generate coherent and contextually appropriate text.

Machine Learning: Machine Learning is a subset of AI that involves training models to learn from data and improve their performance over time without being explicitly programmed. Language models often utilize machine learning techniques to understand and generate text.

Contextual Understanding: Contextual understanding refers to the ability of AI models, particularly language models, to comprehend the meaning of text in the context in which it appears. This includes understanding nuances, recognizing references, and disambiguating ambiguous words or phrases.

Training Data: Training data is the collection of examples or input used to teach AI models. In the case of language models, large datasets of text are used to train the models to understand language patterns and generate coherent responses.

Ethical Considerations: Ethical considerations in AI and LMs involve examining the potential impacts and consequences of their use. This includes addressing issues like bias, fairness, privacy, transparency, and accountability to ensure that AI technologies are developed and used responsibly.

Explainability: Explainability refers to the ability to understand and explain the decision-making process of AI systems, including language models. It is crucial to ensure transparency and build trust by providing insights into how the model arrives at its predictions or generates text.

Bias: Bias in AI refers to the presence of unfair or discriminatory behavior in the outputs or predictions of AI systems. It is essential to address and mitigate bias in language models to avoid perpetuating social, gender, racial, or other forms of bias in generated text.

Data Privacy: Data privacy involves safeguarding sensitive information and ensuring that personal data used to train or interact with AI systems, including language models, is handled securely and in compliance with relevant privacy regulations.

Limitations: It is important to recognize and communicate the limitations of AI systems, including language models, such as their inability to understand context beyond what is explicitly presented or the potential for generating incorrect or misleading information.

Human Oversight: Human oversight involves having human experts or reviewers involved in monitoring, validating, and correcting the outputs of AI systems, including language models, to ensure accuracy, reliability, and adherence to ethical standards.

User Interface: The user interface is the means through which users interact with AI systems, including language models. Designing intuitive and user-friendly interfaces is crucial for effective communication, providing seamless interactions, and enabling users to leverage the capabilities of language models efficiently.

Key issues with AI:

Bias: One problem with AI scraping the internet for data to create its answers, is that it is also scraping the inherent bias that can come with human writing. The classic example is the idea of Columbus discovering America, because this entire idea is based on the eurocentric idea that the native peoples didn't count because they were not European and only Europeans count when it comes to discovering.

Misinformation and hallucinations: Another big problem I have found with using AI is that it frequently hallucinates or makes up answers that aren't true, but they sure sound true. I had a student try to use AI to write a paper once, for example, but he wasn't aware that the AI was hallucination, so he turned it into hallucinations and all. Oops. In the "real world" a lawyer tried to submit a case written by Chat GPT and it was filled with made up information, and the last I heard he was being disbarred as a result. The moral of the story is to be honest, and make sure to at least check multiple sources.

Deep Fakes: Deep fakes are more in the realm of images than language, and the basic idea is that we are at the point where videos can be made to look real that aren't real. You can have the president look like he is rapping or a celebrity look like they are saying something they didn't say in a voice that sounds exactly like theirs. The dark side of this can be seen in the realm of politics, porn, cyber-bullying, etc. In fact, when I hear experts talk on the subject of AI, deep fakes are often cited as one of the most worrisome aspects of AI.

Copyright: To what degree should large AI companies be able to scape the internet for content created by humans without having to pay anything for said content? There is already a lot of pushback around this from companies like Reddit, Getty Images, and others.

Synthetic data: At a certain point, AI is going to have used up all the human created data and it will have to start feeding itself other data created by AI, called "synthetic data," and some studies already suggest this doesn't work very well.

Misinformation: Imagine being able to write an infinite amount of fake news pieces at scale, and churning them out into the universe ad infinitum? How might this affect democracy?

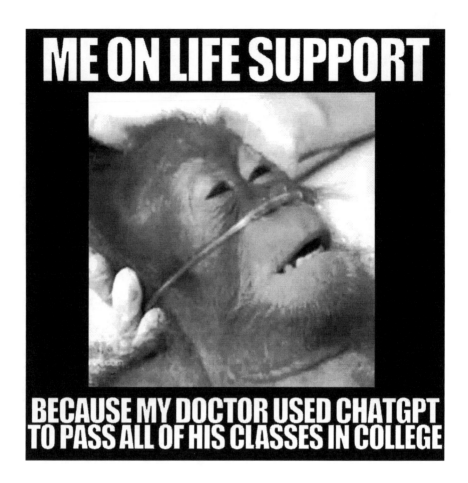

Key questions:

Have you encountered any problems with AI? If so, what were they?

Copyright: If I have AI write a novel or paint a picture, can I copyright it, and make profit from it?

What is the best way to regulate AI? Should the government do it? Should big tech? Should we regulate ourselves? All of the above?

If I had two concepts for you to take away from this class that will help you in life and career, the first would be the distinction between dialectical and dichotomous modes of thinking, and the second would be the concept of framing of an issue:

Read the short handout in The Red Book on Framing:

"People who don't construe their life and don't frame their own tale, stay on the sidelines, remain only an act without a story and turn into an "empty box". Out-of-the-box thinking and inventiveness remains then merely wishful thinking. ("Everybody his story")"

— Erik Pevernagie

"The way we frame our questions shapes the way we see solutions"

-Jerran Gan

Framing and reframing 101:

In the social studies context, framing refers to the way information, issues, or events are presented, structured, or framed by individuals, media, or institutions to influence how people perceive and understand them. Framing involves emphasizing certain aspects of a subject while downplaying or omitting others, which can significantly shape public opinion, attitudes, and responses.

Framing can be found in various forms of communication, such as news articles, political speeches, advertisements, and social media posts. Different frames can be applied to the same topic, leading to different interpretations and understandings of the subject matter.

The concept of framing is closely related to the agenda-setting theory, which suggests that the media and other communication channels not only tell people what to think about but also how to think about it. By controlling the framing of information, individuals or groups can influence public discourse and decision-making processes.

For example, in the context of a political issue, framing could involve presenting a specific policy proposal as either a necessary reform or a dangerous disruption, depending on the desired perception. The framing can influence how individuals perceive the proposal and, consequently, affect their support or opposition to it.

In social studies and related disciplines, researchers often study framing as an important aspect of media analysis, political communication, and public opinion formation. Understanding framing helps individuals become more critical consumers of information and enables scholars to examine how power and persuasion operate in society.

Cognitive reframing, also known as cognitive restructuring, is a psychological technique that involves identifying and then disputing irrational or maladaptive thoughts. The aim is to replace these thoughts with more positive, accurate, or helpful ones. It is a strategy often used in cognitive-behavioral therapy (CBT) and is based on the premise that our perception or interpretation of an event or situation greatly influences our emotional and behavioral responses to it.

In other words, if you can change how you think about or perceive a situation, you can change how you feel and behave in response to it. This technique can be particularly useful in helping individuals cope with stress, anxiety, depression, and other mental health issues. (Open AI)

Here are five examples of cognitive reframing:

Situation: You failed an important test.

Initial thought: "I am a failure. I will never pass this subject."
Reframed thought: "I didn't do well on this test, but that doesn't define my worth. I can learn from my mistakes and improve next time."

Situation: Your friend did not reply to your message immediately.
Initial thought: "They must be ignoring me. They probably don't like me anymore."
Reframed thought: "They might be busy or didn't see my message. I'll give them some time."

Situation: You made a mistake at work.
Initial thought: "I am incompetent. I shouldn't be in this job."
Reframed thought: "Everyone makes mistakes. I can learn from this and use it to improve my skills."

Situation: You were criticized for a presentation you gave.
Initial thought: "I am terrible at public speaking. I should avoid it at all costs."

Reframed thought: "Receiving feedback can help me grow. I can use these comments to get better at public speaking."

Situation: You didn't get a job you interviewed for.
Initial thought: "I am unemployable. No one will ever hire me."
Reframed thought: "Not getting this job doesn't mean I'm not valuable. There are other opportunities out there, and the right job for me is still out there."

Here are five examples of prompts that could help a student come up with their own cognitive reframing examples:

Situation: You got a lower grade than you expected on a project.

Prompt for reframing: Think about how this grade does not reflect your total academic abilities. How can you use this experience to motivate and better prepare yourself for the next project?
Situation: You didn't make it into the team or club you tried out for.

Prompt for reframing: How can you view this situation as a chance to explore other interests or activities you may enjoy?
Situation: You are not able to understand a new topic in class.

Prompt for reframing: Instead of thinking you're not smart enough, how can you see this as an opportunity to develop new learning strategies and resilience?

These prompts are designed to help students practice cognitive reframing and develop healthier thinking habits that can contribute to better mental health and resilience.

See if you can notice an unproductive frame, and reframe into a more productive one.

Situation:
Unproductive frame:
Reframe:

Situation:
Unproductive frame:
Reframe:

Situation:
Unproductive frame:
Reframe:

Situation:
Unproductive frame:
Reframe:

Situation:
Unproductive frame:
Reframe:

Situation:
Unproductive frame:
Reframe:

Repeat this exercise, as necessary, for life!

The concept of how to frame an issue is also critical to academic work as well. Let's look at all the different ways on could frame a paper on the issue of social inequality and democracy:

Social inequality and democracy are expansive topics, and a term paper addressing their interplay could be framed in various ways, depending on the specific angle or aspect the author wishes to explore. Here are several different frameworks:

Historical Analysis:

Title: "The Evolution of Social Inequality in Democratic Societies: A Historical Perspective."
Focus: This paper could trace the historical developments of social inequality in democracies, drawing from examples like ancient Athens, the French Revolution, and modern democratic nations.

Comparative Study:

Title: "Democracy vs. Autocracy: The Impacts on Social Inequality."
Focus: Analyze how different governance structures influence social inequality. Do democracies inherently produce more equality than autocracies, or are there examples to the contrary?
Case Study:

Title: "Social Inequality in Modern Brazil: Challenges to Democratic Governance."
Focus: Dive deep into a specific country's experience, examining the roots of social inequality and the ways in which it challenges or shapes democratic processes.

Economic Lens:
Title: "The Wealth Gap: How Economic Disparities Challenge Democratic Ideals."
Focus: Examine how economic imbalances, especially in wealth and income distribution, can influence democratic participation, representation, and policy outcomes.
Identity and Representation:

Title: "Race, Gender, and Democracy: The Intersections of Identity and Political Participation."
Focus: Explore how various identity factors (like race, gender, religion, etc.) can shape experiences of social inequality in democracies and impact democratic participation.
Institutional Approach:

Title: "The Role of Institutions in Mediating Social Inequality in Democracies."
Focus: Investigate how various democratic institutions, such as electoral systems, judiciaries, or legislative bodies, can either mitigate or exacerbate social inequalities.
Media and Perception:

Title: "Media Narratives and their Impact on Social Inequality in Democratic Societies."
Focus: Explore the role media plays in shaping perceptions of social inequality and how this influences democratic discourse and processes.
Grassroots Movements:

Title: "Grassroots Movements as Agents of Change: Addressing Social Inequality in Democracies."
Focus: Examine the role of grassroots movements, from the Civil Rights Movement in the US to the Yellow Vests in France, in

highlighting and addressing issues of social inequality within democratic structures.
Policy Analysis:

Title: "Policy Responses to Social Inequality: Successes and Failures in Contemporary Democracies."
Focus: Evaluate various policy initiatives aimed at addressing social inequality and assess their effectiveness within democratic contexts.
Future Outlook:

Title: "The Future of Democracy in the Face of Rising Social Inequalities."
Focus: Reflect on current trends in global social inequalities and hypothesize about their potential future impacts on democratic structures and processes.
Each of these frameworks offers a unique lens through which to examine the intricate relationship between social inequality and democracy, allowing for comprehensive exploration and diverse insights.

(Open AI)

Notes, words, concepts, epiphanies and connections:

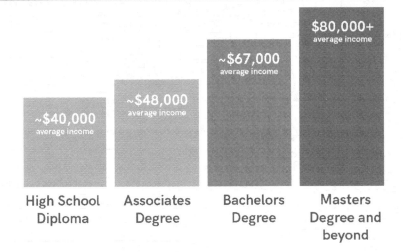

Chapter 3: Education and Learning

Education is the cornerstone of personal development and societal growth. It serves as a vehicle for upward mobility, a bridge to understanding our past and present, and a blueprint for our future. In the United States, the educational landscape has continually evolved, shifting its purpose and priorities in response to changing societal, cultural, economic, and political contexts. This chapter explores the multifaceted and changing purpose of education in the United States. (Open AI)

"Never let school interfere with your education" -Mark Twain

"Education is the most powerful weapon which you can use to change the world." – Nelson Mandela

"The function of education is to teach one to think intensively and to think critically. Intelligence plus character – that is the goal of true education." – Martin Luther King, Jr.

"The beautiful thing about learning is that no one can take it away from you." – B.B. King

"Give a man a fish and you feed him for a day; teach a man to fish and you feed him for a lifetime." – Maimonides

"Education is not the filling of a pail, but the lighting of a fire." – W.B. Yeats

But most of the educational system is quite different. Mass education was designed to turn independent farmers into docile, passive tools of production. That was its primary purpose. And don't think people didn't know it. They knew it and they fought against it. There was a lot of resistance to mass education for exactly that reason. It was also understood by the elites. Emerson once said something about how we're educating them to keep them from our throats. If you don't educate them, what we call "education," they're going to take control — "they" being what Alexander Hamilton called the "great beast," namely the people. The anti-democratic thrust of opinion in what are called democratic societies is really ferocious. And for good reason. Because the freer the society gets, the more dangerous the great beast becomes and the more you have to be careful to cage it somehow. –Noam Chomsky

Overview of public education:

The goals and objectives of public schooling in the U.S. have evolved over the nation's history, reflecting shifts in societal values, economic needs, and political beliefs.

Colonial Era and Early Republic (1600s-1800s):

Goals: The earliest American schools, often single-room schoolhouses, were established by religious groups with the primary purpose of teaching reading, so individuals could study religious texts, particularly the Bible.
Objectives: Promote religious piety, establish moral grounding, and foster basic literacy skills.

Mid to Late 19th Century:

Goals: As the nation grew and industrialized, there was a recognized need for a more educated workforce. The common school movement, led by figures like Horace Mann, advocated for free, universal education as a means to create an informed citizenry.

Objectives: Broaden curriculum to include subjects like mathematics, history, and sciences, ensure greater access to education, and assimilate immigrants into American culture and values.

Early 20th Century:

Goals: The Progressive Era saw a push for schools to adapt to the changing needs of an industrial society. John Dewey and others promoted the idea that schools should reflect and address societal needs and challenges.

Objectives: Implement more child-centered and experiential learning, develop vocational training programs, and focus on social efficiency by preparing students for specific roles in society.

Post-World War II to 1970s:

Goals: In response to the Cold War and the launch of Sputnik by the USSR, there was a push to improve scientific and mathematical instruction to compete globally.

Objectives: Strengthen STEM (Science, Technology, Engineering, Mathematics) education, expand federal funding and involvement in education, and promote equal educational opportunities (e.g., Brown v. Board of Education).

1980s to 2000s:

Goals: Amid concerns about declining academic performance, there was a move toward accountability and standards-based education.

Objectives: Increase standardized testing (e.g., No Child Left Behind Act), establish clear academic standards at state and national levels, and improve the quality of teaching through professional development and alternative certification programs.

21st Century:

Goals: With rapid technological advancements and globalization, there's a push for schools to develop 21st-century skills and ensure that all students, regardless of background, have access to high-quality education.
Objectives: Integrate technology into classrooms, focus on skills like critical thinking, collaboration, and communication, emphasize personalized and differentiated instruction, and address systemic inequities in education.

Throughout its history, the U.S. public education system has continually evolved in its goals and objectives, reflecting broader societal changes and aspirations. While many of these shifts have led to positive reforms and adaptations, challenges remain, and debates about the purpose and direction of public schooling are ongoing.

Where are we now?

Key terms relating to the subject of education:

Curriculum: The planned set of courses, subjects, and learning experiences designed to achieve specific educational goals.

Pedagogy: The method and practice of teaching, including instructional strategies, techniques, and approaches used by educators.

Learning outcomes: The specific knowledge, skills, attitudes, or competencies that students are expected to acquire or demonstrate as a result of their educational experiences.

Bloom's Taxonomy: A hierarchical framework that classifies learning objectives into six levels, ranging from simple recall of information (knowledge) to higher-order thinking skills like analysis, synthesis, and evaluation.

Standardized testing: Assessments administered uniformly to measure student performance and compare it to a predetermined set of standards or benchmarks, often used for accountability and policy decisions.

Inquiry-based learning: An instructional approach that encourages students to actively explore and investigate concepts, posing questions, and seeking answers through research, experimentation, and critical thinking.

Rote-learning:

Digital literacy: The ability to use digital technologies effectively and responsibly, including skills such as information literacy, digital citizenship, online communication, and media literacy.

Critical thinking: The ability to analyze, evaluate, and synthesize information, allowing individuals to make reasoned judgments, solve problems, and engage in thoughtful decision-making.

Cultural competence: The ability to interact effectively and respectfully with individuals from diverse cultural backgrounds, recognizing and valuing differences while promoting inclusivity and understanding.

Metacognition: The awareness and understanding of one's own thought processes, including the ability to plan, monitor, and reflect on learning, leading to improved self-regulation and academic achievement.

Project-based learning: An instructional approach that immerses students in complex, real-world projects, allowing them to explore and apply knowledge and skills through hands-on, collaborative, and interdisciplinary activities.

Key questions:

What should be the purpose of education at primary, secondary, and higher education.

How to improve your reading comprehension:

Passive versus active reading of texts:

When I was in college my roommate would read an entire chapter and highlight everything. He never wrote anything in the margins and when he was finished, I asked him what the chapter was about, and he said, "I have no clue." We laughed, but a lot of people read like this, and thought it might be easier in the moment, but it is more work in the long run. Thus, I would like to make a clear distinction between what I call active and passive reading:

Active Reading Strategies:

There are two primary modes of reading, **active** and **passive.**

Passive reading is like watching television; you just let the words pass by, and take them in without much thought and hoping to be entertained.

Active reading is like having a conversation with a book the way you would with a car salesman who may be trying to sell you a lemon. You keep your crap detector on high, mark down contradictions and questions, challenge things that don't make sense, and still hope to get something of value.

Here are some tips:

1) Do a bit of research before you start reading, get an idea of what you are up against. Read or skim all of the surrounding material such as the introduction, the inside of the dust jacket, the forward, conclusion, etc. Ask yourself what you already know about this subject? Can you relate it to anything in your life experience? It is crucial not to read with an empty head that you are trying to fill, but with a head already full of ideas and experiences that is looking to make connections to what you already know.

2) If, after reading all that, you still don't have an what you're about to read, you may also want to go to the internet and use Wikipedia, AI, or some other source that helps get you started, but

be careful of doing this because the people who write on Wikipedia can be more confusing than the original author or lure your into their interpretation when there may be a better one. AI is much better at simple explanations.

3) As you read the text, keep a running commentary to yourself in the margins to remind yourself of anything you understand, relate to, disagree with, question or simply don't understand. This will make it so that you don't have to re-read the entire text when it's time for an exam, you know what you understand, and where you need help. You can browse your very own Spark notes that have memory devices designed just for you.

4) Don't get bogged down by difficult vocabulary, unless they are KEY TERMS. A key term that the author keeps using so much that if you don't take the time to figure out what it means, you will be wasting your time until you do.

5) By the end of reading the text, you should be able to say what the main point of the text is (thesis). In an academic text, this will usually be restated for you within the last few paragraphs, so pay close attention to what it says there.

6) Once you understand the thesis of a text, and have internalized it enough to put it in your own words, then you should be able to give at least one example that the author uses to support his claim. If you can't think of one from the reading, go back over your text, searching specifically for an example to support whatever claim the author is trying to make. You may need more, depending on the assignment, but the process is the same.

Going back over the text: Try giving difficult passages a close read, but if it still eludes you after reading it two or three times, then try working with another person to figure it out or looking it up. Group work really helps with difficult texts because complex ideas are difficult to articulate and we need somebody else to give us a reality check.

Nota bene: Sometimes the hard work of close reading pays off and you get a really mind blowing idea that was worth the work; other times it will feel like you did a lot of work to figure out something that could be said in a much simpler way. That is just how it is in the land of ideas, but at least you gave your brain a good work out. In addition, the ability to break down complex things is a huge part of what it means to be an intelligent human being.

A note on skimming or speed reading:

Depending on the kind of text you're reading and what your motive is, skimming is an important skill. It means passing your eyes lightly over the page while at the same time looking for specific information or trying to get the basic idea about something. Despite its negative connotation, it is an important skill to have and the more fluent you get at it, the easier it becomes to glean information and put it into context.

Speed Reading or Skimming Overview:

Speed reading is a collection of techniques and strategies aimed at increasing one's reading speed without compromising comprehension. The concept is grounded in the idea that traditional reading habits can be altered or replaced to facilitate faster information processing.

Basic Techniques for Speed Reading:

Minimize Subvocalization: Subvocalization is the habit of silently pronouncing each word we read. While it can help with comprehension for complex texts, it slows down reading. Speed reading involves reducing or eliminating this inner voice, allowing the eyes and brain to process words more quickly.

Use a Pointer or Guide: Move a finger, pen, or pointer along the line as you read. This technique, known as guiding, helps your eyes move smoothly across the text and can increase reading speed.

Chunking: Instead of reading word by word, try to read groups or chunks of words at once. Over time and with practice, you can expand the number of words you process in a single glance.

Expand Peripheral Vision: By training yourself to expand your peripheral vision, you can read multiple words or even whole lines at a glance, reducing the number of eye movements (saccades) and increasing speed.

Reduce Fixations: The eyes naturally pause, or "fixate", on certain words as we read. By consciously reducing these fixations and increasing the amount of information taken in during each pause, you can enhance your reading speed.

Improve Comprehension: Speed reading isn't just about moving quickly through the text—it's crucial to retain comprehension. Continuously practice summarizing content, asking questions about what you've read, and visualizing the information.

Skip Unnecessary Words: With experience, speed readers can identify and skip over less critical words (like "a", "an", "the") without losing comprehension.

Practice Regularly: Like any skill, speed reading improves with consistent practice. Use tools, apps, and exercises specifically designed to enhance speed reading techniques.

Adjust Speed Accordingly: It's essential to recognize that not all content is suitable for speed reading. For instance, complex or dense materials might require a slower, more deliberate pace. Adjust your speed depending on the material and your familiarity with the topic.

Conclusion:

Speed reading can be an invaluable skill, especially in today's information-dense world. However, it's important to strike a balance between speed and comprehension. With dedicated practice and the right techniques, readers can significantly increase their reading speed while retaining a deep understanding of the material (Open AI).

THE KEYS TO THE KINGDOM OF ACADEMIA:
HOW TO WRITE A PROPER SUMMARY.

Writing a good summary is one of the most important things one learns how to do in college and life. Even though it will be tempting to have AI do this for you, the ability to distill a larger work down to its core idea is a seminal skill one needs in order to thrive in an academic and professional setting. Consequently I am going to ask that you use the template below whenever I ask for a summary. To make things clear, I have also broken the summary down into smaller parts to show each integral part, but ultimately your summary should be a nice single paragraph that doesn't exceed a single page double-spaced,

Here is an example of the template for a summary of an academic text entitled, "Social Class and the 'Hidden Curriculum' of Work" by Jean Anyon.

Part 1: The introduction to the work and the central question or issue:

In the work/essay /study /story/. .... by .... he/she/ they .... (tell me what the overall question is, the problem to be solved, the hypothesis to be explored etc.)

In the essay "Social Class and the 'Hidden Curriculum' of Work" by Jean Anyon, she is trying to understand if there is a relevant connection between social class background and the quality of a student's education.

Part 2: Explanation of methodology and definition of any key terms the author uses to answer their question. The methodology, for example, could be statistical data, an allegory, scientific studies / an interview /a personal narrative, a theory, etc.

In order to analyze/answer/study/this, she/he/they

In order to study this, Anyone goes to five different schools in the New Jersey area to observe the teaching of fifth grade students. She labels each school according to how much the parents earn, and labels them accordingly: "working class," "middle class," "affluent professional," and "executive elite." The working class schools, according to Anyon, are comprised of students whose parents work predominantly blue-collar jobs, such as factory workers, waitresses, and salespeople. The executive elite school, on the other hand, is comprised of parents who occupy more white-collar positions such as doctors, lawyers, and CEOs of major corporations.

Part 3: Paraphrase the author's thesis or conclusion in your own words.

The author/ Anyon /she concludes / argues / contends /

Anyon contends that there is a qualitative difference in the way students are taught according to social class. In the working class schools, for example, the students are mostly taught to follow directions and keep busy. They get in trouble for asking questions or thinking outside of the intellectual parameters set up by the instructor. Conversely, at the executive elite school, the fifth grade students were asked to do complex analytical thinking such as looking at the "elements that make up a civilization," and "comparing the way the citizens of Athens choose their leaders compared to ours (Anyon 12). She suggests that since the working class kids are taught mostly how to listen and follow directions and the executive elite kids are taught more how to use critical thinking skills, this could contribute to keeping students working jobs that keep them within their social class because that is what they have been prepared for. Therefore, she argues more research should be done to see if this is the case.

End with a quote that basically says what you just paraphrased.

As Anyon states, "The identification of different emphasis in classrooms in a sample of contrasting social-class contexts implies that further research should conducted in a large number of schools..." (20)

Here is the beautiful summary each of these parts creates:

In the essay "Social Class and the 'Hidden Curriculum' of Work" by Jean Anyon, she is trying to understand if there is a relevant connection between social class background and the quality of a student's education. In order to investigate this, Anyon goes to five different schools in the New Jersey area to observe the teaching of fifth grade students. She labels each school according to how much the parents earn, and labels them accordingly: "working class," "middle class," "affluent professional," and "executive elite." The working class schools, according to Anyon, are comprised of students whose parents work predominantly blue-collar jobs, such as factory workers, waitresses, and salespeople. The executive elite school, on the other hand, is comprised of parents who occupy more white-collar positions such as doctors, lawyers, and CEO's of major corporations. Anyon contends that there is a qualitative difference in the way students are taught according to social class. In the working class schools, for example, the students are mostly taught to follow directions and keep busy. They get in trouble for asking questions or thinking outside of the intellectual parameters set up by the instructor. Conversely, at the executive elite school, the fifth grade students were asked to do complex analytical thinking such as looking the "elements that make up a civilization," and "comparing the way the citizens of Athens choose their leaders compared to ours (Anyon 12). She suggest that since the working class kids are taught mostly how to listen and follow directions and the executive elite kids are taught more how to use critical thinking skills, this could contribute to keeping students working jobs that keep them within their social class because that is what they have been prepared for. Therefore, she argues more research should be done to see if this is the case. As Anyon states, "The identification of different emphasis in classrooms in a sample of contrasting social-class contexts implies that further research should conducted in a large number of schools..." (20)

Critical notes for writing a summary:

1) A summary should be 90% your paraphrasing of the work, and only 10% quoting of the text at the end. Please don't cut and paste your way to a summary.

2) When you introduce a key term from a text you only have to put it in quotes once to let the reader know.

3) When you put a key word in quotes, please put the punctuation INSIDE the quote. For example, Anyon went to a "working class," and "executive elite" school in New Jersey. VS the wrong way which is, Anyon went to a "working class", and executive elite school in New Jersey. In England they put a comma outside the quote, but not in the good old USA.

4) Titles to books, films, and newspapers should be underlined or *italicized*, but essays, short stories and poems are put in "Quotations."

5) After you say the author's full name at the start, use only their last name from then on.

You would say, Anyon says… and not Jean says…

6) If you introduce a direct quote with the name of the author, you only have to put the page number at the end of the quote to indicate where it is from, such as:

As Anyon writes, "There is a qualitative difference here" (5).

If you don't put their name in the introduction, then you have to put it at the end with the page number, such as:

The results were drastic. "There is a qualitative difference here" (Anyon 5)

7) If you only want part of a direct quote because it is too long for your purposes, you can simply use an ellipsis… to indicate a part is missing.

Anyon writes "…more research is needed" (5).

Or

Anyon concludes, "The qualitative difference was profound…" (7).

Finally, just a basic thing to keep in mind when writing a summary is to imagine having to tell somebody what a text is about using your words in the most concise and efficient way possible.

In addition to summarizing a text I will also sometimes also ask to you do the following:

Identify the motive: Why do you think the author created this text, and what do they hope you will do with the information they provided.

I think the author wrote this essay to expose the inequality of curriculum that exists within the system in the hope of changing it, so that everyone is given a more executive elite education.

Make a personal connection to the material so that it connects to your pre-existing neural pathways: Can you relate to what the author is talking about on a personal level, either from lived experience or ideas you have thought about in another context?

There are two ways you can do this:

1) Life experience example: After reading Anyon, I can say that the majority of my classes in elementary school and high school (and many in college as well) related to the working class and middle class schools. I remember very clearly filling out worksheets, and doing mindless tasks in most of my classes. There were exceptions, however, such as an English teacher I had in my sophomore year

who got us to write our own poems, lead classroom discussion, and be much more engaged in the process of learning.

2) Other idea example:

The idea of unequal education is also exemplified in Jonathan Kozal's book Savage Inequalities, where he looks at the qualitative difference in education at different schools, not only along the lines of class but also race. The book illuminates the vast gaps in funding, resources, and opportunities between schools in affluent and impoverished communities. In wealthier schools, Kozol found modern facilities, well-paid and motivated teachers, and a robust curriculum. In contrast, he found schools in poorer neighborhoods characterized by dilapidated facilities, underpaid and often less qualified teachers, inadequate materials and resources, and a narrow, test-driven curriculum.

Critical thinking question: What part of this text did you find the most confusing, untenable, or something you might disagree with? How do you think the author would respond to your question? What would you say in response?

The main issues I have with this essay is that it is very dated, and the sample size of the schools is so small as to be almost anecdotal. In addition, the examples feel almost cherry-picked at times in order to corroborate her thesis; an example of this would be when she describes how the elite students are creating pyramids of power to examine the structures of power in society. This could all be coincidental, of course, but it felt somewhat preachy at times. If I were to bring these issues to Anyon, I think the first thing she would say is that she admits it this is a small sample group at the end of the essay when she explicitly that "more research is needed," and I would agree. In regard to my critique of cherry, I think she would probably say that she wrote down what she saw, and that the examples are true. If there were any bias, she might say, it was subconscious. In the end, I might agree with this since the examples she gives are very resonant with experiences I have had in my own education, which ultimately why I continue to assign this reading despite it's age and its scientifically dubious quality. The fact is that many students are still being taught in ways similar to those described in the affluent professional and executive elite category.

Notes, words, concepts, epipahnies and connections:

Chapter 4: Economics part 1 Capitalism

As an English major, I never took Economics in college, but as an instructor who is tasked with teaching critical thinking, I realized that critical thinking is all about understanding power, and without understanding money, it's hard to understand power. Thus, I have tried to include a basic primer of economic principles so that we can begin to understand how money and power work together, and what better way to start than with a basic understanding of capitalism.

The study of economics delves into the intricate web of human interactions, choices, and resource allocation within societies. It explores how individuals, businesses, governments, and nations make decisions regarding the production, distribution, and consumption of goods and services. Economics analyzes the forces of supply and demand, market dynamics, and the impact of policies and institutions on the economy. It encompasses a wide range of topics, including microeconomics, which focuses on individual agents and markets, and macroeconomics, which examines the broader aspects of aggregate economic phenomena such as inflation, unemployment, and economic growth. Studying economics equips individuals with a framework to understand the complexities of the global economy, evaluate trade-offs, analyze data, and develop informed insights into economic phenomena. It offers valuable insights into the mechanisms that shape our world, guiding policymakers, businesses, and individuals in making rational decisions to promote prosperity and address societal challenges. (Open AI)

To understand the basics of economics, it is important to be familiar with key terms and concepts that underpin the economic system.

Key terms for economics part 1:

Let's start with a short paragraph about capitalism:

Capitalism is an economic system characterized by private ownership of production means, where investment, production, distribution, income, and prices are determined through a free market. It began to take shape in Europe during the 16th and 17th centuries, with mercantilism laying its early foundations. The 18th and 19th centuries' Industrial Revolution marked a significant turning point, with technological innovations allowing mass production and a shift from agrarian to industrial economies. Influential economists like Adam Smith advocated for free markets and limited government intervention, principles central to capitalist ideology. In the 20th century, capitalism continued to evolve and spread globally, leading to different variants, globalization, and ongoing debates about challenges such as income inequality and environmental sustainability (Open AI).

Paraphrasing means looking at a text and rewriting it in your own words as you try to preserve the most important points:

Here is an example:
Adam Smith - The Wealth of Nations

Capitalism is a free market system where businesses **compete for profit** through production, investment, and distribution of products and services. It has its roots in mercantilism and really began to expand during the industrial revolutions of the 18th and 19th centuries. Adam Smith is one of the first to write extensively about it, and it has continued to change since then in both its scope and purpose.

Note: It is possible to paraphrase something and still not really understand what you are talking about. Maybe you don't know what mercantilism is, for example, but you can still include it in your paraphrase, but you should also note it is important to know what this means if you really want to understand your subject. This is why I am always stressing the importance of keywords. You will find more below:

Capital: Financial assets, wealth, or resources that are used to invest in and generate further economic activity. Capital includes money, physical assets (such as machinery or buildings), and intellectual property.

Private property: Ownership rights and control over assets, goods, or resources that are not owned or controlled by the government. Private property is a fundamental aspect of capitalism, allowing individuals and businesses to own, trade, and accumulate wealth.

Why do you need private property for capitalism to work?

Natural resources

Labor

Supply and demand

Marketing

Intellectual property

Industrial Revolution

The means of production

Market economy : (See Capitalism)

Profit motive: The driving force behind economic activity in capitalism, where individuals and businesses aim to maximize their profits or financial gains by efficiently producing and selling goods or services.

Free enterprise: The freedom for individuals and businesses to engage in economic activities with limited government regulation. It allows for entrepreneurial initiative, competition, and the pursuit of profit within legal and ethical boundaries.

Competition: The rivalry among businesses or individuals seeking to gain market share, customers, and profits.

After many years of trying to understand the relationship between politics and money, I have found that the heart of this battle is always between the desire for capitalists to make a profit, and the desire of the government to regulate those profits for one reason or another. Keep in mind that corporations often use the government to regulate things on their own behalf through things like lobbying for tax breaks, government defense contracts, and intellectual property enforcement, regulation and capitalism are still the key to understanding the fight between profit and democracy, which is one of the most important issues of our time.

Government regulation refers to the rules, laws, and standards set by the government or its authorized bodies to govern the behavior of individuals, businesses, and other entities within a society. These regulations are typically established to protect the welfare of the public, ensure market competition, and promote societal objectives like environmental protection, public health, and safety.

Examples of Government Regulation:

Labor Regulations: Laws that protect the worker for things like minimum wage, working conditions, child labor laws.

Unions: A labor union, often simply referred to as a "union," is an organization of workers who have come together to achieve common goals, such as protecting the integrity of their trade, improving safety standards, achieving higher pay and benefits, and better working conditions.

Collective bargaining:

Representatives of the union negotiate with employers on behalf of the union members to reach an agreement on terms of employment, such as wages, work hours, health and safety conditions, and other job-related matters. The resulting agreement is known as a collective bargaining agreement (CBA).

Strikes: negotiations break down or if workers feel that their rights are being violated, a union may organize a strike, where workers stop working in an effort to pressurize the employer to meet their demands.

Environmental Regulations: Laws that protect the environment by regulating pollution levels, waste management, and natural resource use. For instance, the Clean Air Act in the U.S. regulates the emission of pollutants from factories, vehicles, and other sources to maintain air quality.

Consumer Protection: Rules that ensure the rights of consumers are protected against fraudulent business practices. For example, regulations might require businesses to provide accurate labeling of food products, including nutritional information and ingredients.

Banking and Finance: Regulations that govern the operations of financial institutions to ensure financial stability and protect consumers. The Dodd-Frank Wall Street Reform and Consumer Protection Act in the U.S., for example, was enacted after the 2008 financial crisis to reduce risks in the financial system.

Health and Safety: Rules that set standards to ensure safe working conditions and public health. Occupational Safety and Health Administration (OSHA) standards in the U.S. regulate workplace environments to prevent worker injuries and illnesses.

Medicine and Pharmaceuticals: Regulations like the approval process for new drugs by agencies such as the U.S. Food and Drug Administration (FDA) to ensure the safety and efficacy of medical treatments available to the public.

Agriculture: Standards and subsidies that may affect farming practices, pesticide use, and animal husbandry. For example, some governments may provide subsidies to promote organic farming or enact regulations to ensure humane treatment of livestock.

In short, if you are a CEO of a corporation, your job is to maximize profits for your shareholders, and so it would be in your best interest to oppose government regulations. This is what is known as laissez-faire capitalism, which means "hands off" in French, which means the government should keep the hands off our ability to make profit.

There are a variety of names for this same concept which I shall list below:

Laissez-faire: A concept advocating minimal government interference or regulation in economic affairs. It suggests that markets should operate freely without excessive government control, allowing individuals and businesses to make their own decisions.

Bottom line thinking: How does this affect our profits? The bottom line = profit margin

Supply side economics
Neoliberal economics
Trickle down economics
Supply side economics

Many argue that this idea of trickle down economics hasn't worked and has led to income inequality, especially with the rise of the modern corporation.

Income inequality: The unequal distribution of income or wealth within a society. In capitalist systems, income inequality can arise due to variations in individuals' skills, education, market demand for different occupations, and other factors.
Late stage capitalism: a term used to describe the current stage of capitalism, marked by things such as the increase of income inequality, and rampant consumerism. The term is used frequently in memes and jokes when describing why one's life sucks, "It's late stage capitalism."

Notes, words, concepts, epiphanies, ideas and connections:

Economics part 2

The Corporation

To study the massive influence of corporations on modern global society is a massive undertaking, as it is at the heart of almost every major issue facing the world. Because this is a humanities class, we focus more on the downside of corporations and the impact they have on labor, the environment, and natural resources. In a business class, you would focus on the positive aspects of a corporation as an entity to help grow profits and expand markets at a rapid pace. I think it is important to understand both sides of this debate in order to make more informed decisions both as a member of a democracy as well as a business person.

The modern corporation is a legal entity separate from its owners, created to conduct business, and characterized by structures such as shareholders, a board of directors, and management. Originating in medieval Europe with chartered companies like the British East India Company, the corporate form underwent significant growth in the 19th century with the introduction of limited liability, encouraging more investments. The 20th century marked a global expansion of corporations, leading to the rise of multinational entities, a push back against regulation, and unprecedented power and influence. Corporations are legally bound to make profits for their shareholders, but have recently tried to rebrand themselves from being greedy monsters to stewards of the planet who care about the environment, labor, and diversity. This issue is highly controversial and is at the heart of the eternal battle between profits and democracy (Open AI).

Paraphrase the aforementioned paragraph in your own words:

If you only know two things about a corporation, they should be the following:

1) They are legally bound to increase profits for their shareholders.

2) They have limited liability, which means that you can sue a corporation, but you can't sue the individual shareholders. They are protected by the corporation.

Here are more important terms to understand corporations:

CEO (Chief Executive Officer): The top executive in a corporation who is responsible for managing the company's overall operations, implementing strategies, and making key decisions. The CEO reports to the board of directors.

Public company: A corporation whose shares are publicly traded on a stock exchange or sold to the general public. Public companies are subject to regulatory requirements and provide financial disclosures, allowing anyone to become a shareholder.

Stock market: A platform or exchange where shares of publicly-traded companies are bought and sold. The stock market provides a mechanism for companies to raise capital and investors to buy and sell ownership stakes in businesses.

Shareholder: An individual or entity that owns shares or stock in a corporation, representing a partial ownership interest in the company. Shareholders have rights, such as voting on corporate matters and receiving dividends.

Stakeholder:

Board of Directors: A group of individuals elected or appointed to represent shareholders and oversee the management and strategic decision-making of a corporation. The board sets policies, appoints executives, and ensures the company's long-term viability.

Merger and Acquisition (M&A): The consolidation of companies through various transactions, such as mergers (combining two companies into one) or acquisitions (one company acquiring another). M&A activities are common among corporations and can have significant implications for market competition and industry dynamics.

Corporate Culture: The shared values, beliefs, norms, and behaviors that shape the identity and working environment within a corporation. Corporate culture influences employee behavior, decision-making, and the overall organizational climate.

Innovation: innovation refers to the process of creating, developing, and implementing a new product, process, service, or idea with the aim of improving efficiency, effectiveness, or competitive advantage. Innovation can be incremental, radical, or disruptive, depending on the degree of change it brings about.

The Dark Side of Corporations key concepts:

"I hope that we shall crush in its birth the aristocracy of our monied corporations which dare already to challenge our government to a trial of strength, and bid defiance to the laws of our country."

— Thomas Jefferson, The Papers of Thomas Jefferson: Retirement Series, Volume 10: 1 May 1816 to 18 January 1817

"Surely by now there can be few here who still believe the purpose of government is to protect us from the destructive activities of corporations. At last most of us must understand that the opposite is true: that the primary purpose of the government is to protect those who run the economy from the outrage of injured citizens."

— Derrick Jensen, Endgame, Vol. 1: The Problem of Civilization

Monopoly: A market structure where a single company or entity has exclusive control over the supply of a particular product or service, often resulting in limited competition. Monopolies can have implications for market efficiency and consumer welfare.

Nepotism: Favoritism shown to relatives or close associates in the hiring, promotion, or awarding of contracts, often disregarding merit or qualifications.

Lobbying: The practice of influencing government officials or legislators to shape policies or laws in favor of a particular company or industry, sometimes through questionable means.

Conflict of Interest: A situation where an individual's personal interests or relationships could potentially compromise their ability to act impartially or in the best interests of an organization.

Corporate Fraud: Deceptive or dishonest activities carried out by individuals or groups within a corporation, often for personal gain, resulting in financial loss or harm to stakeholders.

Cartel: An association of companies or businesses that collude to control and manipulate market prices, restrict competition, and allocate market share, typically to their mutual benefit.

Offshore Accounts: Bank accounts or financial entities established in low-tax or tax-haven jurisdictions to facilitate illicit activities, evade taxes, or conceal assets.

Regulatory Capture: The phenomenon where regulatory agencies, responsible for overseeing industries and enforcing regulations, become influenced or controlled by the entities they are meant to regulate, leading to a lack of effective oversight.

This could also be described as the old fox guarding the hen house analogy.

Ponzi Scheme: A fraudulent investment scheme where early investors are paid returns using funds from subsequent investors rather than from legitimate profits, eventually collapsing when new investments dry up.

Corporate Culture: The shared values, attitudes, norms, and behaviors within an organization, which can either foster integrity, ethical behavior, and transparency or contribute to a culture of corruption and misconduct.

Corporation: A legally recognized entity or business structure that is separate and distinct from its owners or shareholders. Corporations have rights and liabilities, and they are typically formed to conduct business activities and generate profits.

Insider Trading: The illegal practice of trading stocks based on material nonpublic information, giving individuals an unfair advantage over other market participants.

Pump and Dump: A fraudulent scheme where individuals or groups artificially inflate the price of a stock by spreading false or misleading information to attract investors, only to sell their shares at the elevated price before the inevitable collapse.

Inside Information: see insider trading

Greenwashing: A deceptive marketing practice where a company exaggerates or falsely claims its products or policies are environmentally friendly to appeal to green-minded consumers.

Example: A company markets its product as "eco-friendly" because it has a small amount of recycled material, even though its production process is harmful to the environment.

Outsourcing: The practice of hiring external organizations or individuals, often from other countries, to perform certain tasks, services, or manufacturing processes.

Example: A tech company based in the U.S. might outsource its customer support operations to a call center in the Philippines.

The Race to the Bottom: A competitive situation where companies or nations shop around the globe for places to do business where there are lower standards for things like wages, quality, or environmental regulations in order to attract business or investment at the expense of broader societal interests.

Example: Countries might lower environmental regulations to attract manufacturing businesses, resulting in increased pollution.

Automation: The use of technology, especially computer systems, robots, or artificial intelligence, to control and perform tasks that previously required human intervention.

Example: Car manufacturing plants using robots to assemble vehicles.

Social Darwinism: A belief that the principles of natural selection apply to human societies, often used to justify societal inequalities and the idea that the strong see their wealth and power increase while the weak see their wealth and power decrease.

Example: Arguments in the 19th century that imperial powers had the right to dominate "lesser" nations based on their supposed natural superiority.

Intellectual Property: Creations of the mind, such as inventions, literary and artistic works, symbols, names, and images used in commerce, for which exclusive rights are recognized.
Example: A software developer patents a new application they've created.

Reverse Engineering: The process of disassembling and analyzing a product or system to understand its components, architecture, and design, often to replicate or improve upon it.
Example: A tech company takes apart a competitor's smartphone to understand its hardware design.

Privatization: The process of transferring ownership of a business, enterprise, agency, or public service from the public sector (government) to the private sector (businesses or individuals).
Example: A government-owned water supply company being sold to a private entity.

Government Subsidies: Financial aid, support, or tax breaks given by the government to promote certain industries, reduce the prices of products or services, or achieve other policy goals. Subsidies can sometimes be misused or misallocated, leading to corruption or favoritism. If a certain industry or company receives subsidies due to lobbying efforts rather than genuine public benefit, it can erode trust in the system.

Advanced terms for financial and stock market fraud for those interested:

Wash Trading: The practice of artificially creating trading activity by buying and selling the same security simultaneously or in rapid succession to give the appearance of legitimate trading volume and price movement.

Churning: Excessive buying and selling of securities within a client's account by a broker to generate excessive commissions, often at the expense of the investor's best interests.

Short and Distort: A strategy where an individual or group takes a short position in a stock and then spreads false or negative information about the company, hoping to drive down the stock price and profit from the decline.

Spoofing: A manipulative tactic in which traders place large orders with the intention of canceling them before they are executed, creating a false impression of market demand or supply.

Bear Raid: An attempt by investors or traders to drive down the price of a stock by aggressively selling it short, often through coordinated efforts and spreading negative sentiment about the company.

High-Frequency Trading (HFT): The use of sophisticated algorithms and high-speed computer systems to execute a large number of trades in fractions of a second, exploiting minute price discrepancies for quick profits.

Boiler Room Operations: Unscrupulous brokerage firms that employ aggressive and often fraudulent sales tactics to pressure individuals into buying or selling securities, often of dubious quality or value.

Notes, epiphanies, ideas, words and connections:

Chapter 5: Politics and Government

Politics can be a very daunting subject as it is often divisive, and insights dichotomous thinking. It is imperative, however, to have some understanding of politics in order to be a critical thinker, and part of a functioning democracy. Without a basic understanding of politics, it is impossible to understand the key power dynamics in society that shape both our personal and public lives. As with any subject, there are many degrees of understanding, but our goal is to have a basic overview that will prime you for cocktail parties, podcasts, and further study if it interests you.

The study of political science opens the door to a captivating exploration of power, governance, and the dynamics of societies. It seeks to understand the intricate workings of political systems, institutions, and the behavior of individuals and groups within them. Political science delves into the realm of public policy, international relations, comparative politics, and political theory, offering a comprehensive lens through which we can analyze and interpret the complex political landscape. By studying political science, we gain insights into the distribution of power, the formation of political ideologies, the influence of public opinion, and the impact of policies on societies. It equips us with the tools to critically evaluate political events, understand the processes of decision-making, and engage in informed discussions about the challenges and opportunities facing our world. The study of political science is not only intellectually stimulating but also crucial for navigating the complexities of governance and shaping a better future for societies worldwide (Open AI).

"On the whole human beings want to be good, but not too good, and not quite all the time."

— George Orwell, All Art is Propaganda: Critical Essays

"In each of us, two natures are at war – the good and the evil. All our lives the fight goes on between them, and one of them must conquer. But in our own hands lies the power to choose – what we want most to be we are."

— Robert Louis Stevenson

. "Hate does that. Burns off everything but itself, so whatever your grievance is, your face looks just like your enemy's." – Toni Morrison, Love

In order to understand the root of politics and argument better, it is imperative to look first at the concept of human nature.

Human nature, a concept that has intrigued philosophers, scientists, historians, and theologians for centuries, refers to the distinctive characteristics—including ways of thinking, feeling, and acting—that humans tend to have naturally. This notion raises fundamental questions about who we are, why we behave the way we do, and how intrinsic aspects of our being might be shaped by biology and history.

Many theories have been posited to explain human nature:

Philosophical Perspectives: Philosophers like Plato believed in the existence of an eternal soul, while others, such as Thomas Hobbes, viewed humans as essentially selfish and brutish in a state of nature.

Biological Perspectives: Evolutionary biology suggests that certain traits in humans have been selected for over time because they provided survival and reproductive advantages. Traits like cooperation, empathy, and even our propensity for creating culture may have evolutionary underpinnings.

Cultural and Sociological Perspectives: While biology might give us a framework, culture shapes how we express our instincts and desires. Humans are social creatures, and the societies we construct can influence our behavior, values, and perceptions.

Theological Perspectives: Many world religions offer views on human nature, often presenting ideas about the inherent goodness or sinfulness of humans and how one should lead a virtuous life.

While discussions about human nature can often lead to more questions than answers, what remains clear is that humans are a complex interplay of biology and culture. The quest to understand our nature is intrinsic to our desire to understand our place in the world and the essence of what makes us uniquely human.

"The liberty of a democracy is not safe if the people tolerate the growth of private power to a point where it becomes stronger than the democratic state itself. That in its essence is fascism: ownership of government by an individual, by a group, or any controlling private power."

— Franklin D. Roosevelt

"Well first of all, tell me: Is there some society you know that doesn't run on greed? You think Russia doesn't run on greed? You think China doesn't run on greed? What is greed? Of course, none of us are greedy, it's only the other fellow who's greedy. The world runs on individuals pursuing their separate interests. The great achievements of civilization have not come from government bureaus. Einstein didn't construct his theory under order from a bureaucrat. Henry Ford didn't revolutionize the automobile industry that way. In the only cases in which the masses have escaped from the kind of grinding poverty you're talking about, the only cases in recorded history are where they have had capitalism and largely free trade. If you want to know where the masses are worse off, worst off, it's exactly in the kinds of societies that depart from that. So that the record of history is absolutely crystal clear, that there is no alternative way so far discovered of improving the lot of the ordinary people that can hold a candle to the productive activities that are unleashed by the free-enterprise system."

–Milton Freidman

"The essence of capitalism is to turn nature into commodities and commodities into capital. The live green earth is transformed into dead gold bricks, with luxury items for the few and toxic slag heaps for the many. The glittering mansion overlooks a vast sprawl of shanty towns, wherein a desperate, demoralized humanity is kept in line with drugs, television, and armed force."

— Michael Parenti, Against Empire

"Socialism is a philosophy of failure, the creed of ignorance, and the gospel of envy, its inherent virtue is the equal sharing of misery."

-Winston Churchhill

In a society governed passively by free markets and free elections, organized greed always defeats disorganized democracy."

— Matt Taibbi, Griftopia: Bubble Machines, Vampire Squids, and the Long Con That Is Breaking America

To understand politics, here are twenty keywords that are essential to grasp the dynamics and concepts within the field:

Government: The system or body that exercises political authority and governs a country or region.

Politics

Political spectrum

Continuum

Egalitarian

Hierarchical

Democracy: A form of government where power rests with the people, who either directly participate in decision-making or elect representatives to make decisions on their behalf.

Direct democracy

Representative democracy

Constitution: A fundamental document that establishes the basic principles, rights, and structure of a government or organization.

Political Party: An organized group of individuals with shared political beliefs and objectives that seeks to gain and exercise political power through elections.

Ideology: A system of beliefs, values, and ideas that shapes political thought and influences policy decisions. Examples include liberalism, conservatism, socialism, and nationalism.

Legislature: A branch of government responsible for making laws. It is usually composed of elected representatives, such as a parliament or congress.

Executive: A branch of government responsible for implementing and enforcing laws. It is typically led by a president, prime minister, or monarch.

Judiciary: The branch of government responsible for interpreting laws and ensuring their constitutionality. It includes courts and judges.

Political System: The framework of institutions, processes, and rules that govern political behavior and decision-making within a society.

Elections: The process by which citizens choose their representatives or leaders through voting.

Policy: A course of action or set of principles adopted and pursued by a government or political entity to address specific issues or achieve particular goals.

Power: The ability or capacity to influence or control political decisions and outcomes.

Diplomacy: The practice of conducting negotiations and maintaining relations between countries or political entities.

Political Activism: Engaging in activities and actions aimed at influencing political change or raising awareness about specific issues.

Civil Liberties: Basic individual rights and freedoms protected by law, such as freedom of speech, assembly, and religion.

Public Opinion: The collective views, attitudes, and beliefs of the general public on political issues and events.

Monarchy: A form of government in which a single individual, usually a hereditary monarch, serves as the head of state. Monarchs have varying levels of power, from ceremonial roles to absolute authority.

Republic: A system where the country's sovereignty resides in the people, and the head of state is an elected or appointed official, rather than a monarch. Republics may have a president, prime minister, or other designated leaders.

Authoritarianism: A system where power is concentrated in a single ruler or a small group without meaningful democratic processes or checks and balances. Authoritarian governments often suppress political opposition and limit civil liberties.

Totalitarianism: An extreme form of authoritarianism where the government exercises complete control over all aspects of public and private life, suppressing dissent and imposing strict ideological conformity.

Dictatorship: A government in which power is held by an individual who wields supreme authority, often acquired and maintained through force or coercion.

Theocracy: A system where religious leaders hold political power, and religious law serves as the basis for governance.

Plutocracy

Oligarchy: A form of government in which a small group of individuals or families controls political power, often based on wealth, social status, or military influence.

Anarchy: A theoretical state of society without a government or central authority. Anarchy is characterized by the absence of hierarchical control and the belief in self-governance.

Libertarian

Karl Marx

Marxism: A social, political, and economic theory developed by Karl Marx and Friedrich Engels, emphasizing the struggle between the working class (proletariat) and the owning class (bourgeoisie) and advocating for a classless society.

Proletariat: The working class, those who sell their labor for wages and do not own the means of production.

Bourgeoisie: The capitalist class, the owners of capital, land, and industry who exploit the labor of the proletariat for profit.

Class Struggle: The ongoing conflict and antagonism between the proletariat and the bourgeoisie, driven by their opposing economic interests.

Surplus Value: The value produced by workers that exceeds the wages paid to them, which is appropriated by the capitalist as profit.

Alienation: The feeling of separation or estrangement experienced by workers under capitalism, resulting from their loss of control over the products of their labor and their exploitation by the capitalist class.

Means of Production: The resources, tools, machinery, and infrastructure necessary for the production of goods and services.

Communism: The ultimate goal of Marxism, representing a classless, stateless society where the means of production are owned collectively and wealth is distributed based on need.

Socialist State: A transitional stage between capitalism and communism, where the state plays a role in the ownership and control of the means of production, working towards the eventual establishment of communism.

Imperialism: The expansionist policies and practices of capitalist nations, involving the colonization, domination, and exploitation of other countries and regions for economic and political gain.

Revolution: A radical and transformative change in the social, political, or economic structure of society, often associated with the overthrow of existing power structures.

Class Consciousness: The awareness among members of a social class of their shared interests, common oppression, and the need for collective action.

Top down communism

Bottom up communism

Right wing / Conservative

Left wing / Liberal

Far right / alt right

Far left

Fascism

Socialism

Mixed economy / market socialism

Social democrat

"Look, America is no more a democracy than Russia is a Communist state. The governments of the U.S. and Russia are practically the same. There's only a difference of degree. We both have the same basic form of government: economic totalitarianism. In other words, the settlement to all questions, the solutions to all issues are determined not by what will make the people most healthy and happy in the bodies and their minds but by economics. Dollars or rubles. Economy uber alles. Let nothing interfere with economic growth, even though that growth is castrating truth, poisoning beauty, turning a continent into a shit-heap and driving an entire civilization insane. Don't spill the Coca-Cola, boys, and keep those monthly payments coming."

— Tom Robbins, Another Roadside Attraction

"The Master said, "If your conduct is determined solely by considerations of profit you will arouse great resentment."
— Confucius

"The superior man understands what is right; the inferior man understands what will sell."
— Confucius

"He tried to read an elementary economics text; it bored him past endurance, it was like listening to somebody interminably recounting a long and stupid dream. He could not force himself to understand how banks functioned and so forth, because all the operations of capitalism were as meaningless to him as the rites of a primitive religion, as barbaric, as elaborate, and as unnecessary. In a human sacrifice to deity there might be at least a mistaken and terrible beauty; in the rites of the moneychangers,

where greed, laziness, and envy were assumed to move all men's acts, even the terrible became banal."
— Ursula K. Le Guin, The Dispossessed: An Ambiguous Utopia

"In a society governed passively by free markets and free elections, organized greed always defeats disorganized democracy."
— Matt Taibbi, Griftopia: Bubble Machines, Vampire Squids, and the Long Con That Is Breaking America

"Look, America is no more a democracy than Russia is a Communist state. The governments of the U.S. and Russia are practically the same. There's only a difference of degree. We both have the same basic form of government: economic totalitarianism. In other words, the settlement to all questions, the solutions to all issues are determined not by what will make the people most healthy and happy in the bodies and their minds but by economics. Dollars or rubles. Economy uber alles. Let nothing interfere with economic growth, even though that growth is castrating truth, poisoning beauty, turning a continent into a shit-heap and driving an entire civilization insane. Don't spill the Coca-Cola, boys, and keep those monthly payments coming."

— Tom Robbins, Another Roadside Attraction

"The most dangerous people in the world are not the tiny minority instigating evil acts, but those who do the acts for them. For example, when the British invaded India, many Indians accepted to work for the British to kill off Indians who resisted their occupation. So in other words, many Indians were hired to kill other Indians on behalf of the enemy for a paycheck. Today, we have mercenaries in Africa, corporate armies from the western world, and unemployed men throughout the Middle East killing their own people - and people of other nations - for a paycheck. To act without a conscience, but for a paycheck, makes anyone a dangerous animal. The devil would be powerless if he couldn't entice people to do his work. So as long as money continues to seduce the hungry, the hopeless, the broken, the greedy, and the needy, there will always be war between brothers."

— Suzy Kassem

America is the greatest engine of innovation that has ever existed, and it can't be duplicated anytime soon, because it is the product of a multitude of factors: extreme freedom of thought, an emphasis on independent thinking, a steady immigration of new minds, a risk-taking culture with no stigma attached to trying and failing, a non corrupt bureaucracy, and financial markets and a venture capital system that are unrivaled at taking new ideas and turning them into global products."

Thomas L Freidman

"It's easier to imagine the end of the world than the end of capitalism."

Mark Fischer

"Modern capitalism needs men who co-operate smoothly, and in large numbers; who want to consume more and more; and whose tastes are standardized and can be easily influenced and anticipated. It needs men who feel free and independent, not subject to any authority or principle or conscience—yet willing to be commanded, to do what is expected of them, to fit into the social machine without friction; who can be guided without force, led without leaders, prompted without aim—except the one to make good, to be on the move, to function, to go ahead. What is the outcome? Modern man is alienated from himself, from his fellow men, and from nature."

— Erich Fromm, The Art of Loving

"It's true: greed has had a very bad press. I frankly don't see anything wrong with greed. I think that the people who are always attacking greed would be more consistent with their position if they refused their next salary increase. I don't see even the most Left-Wing scholar in this country scornfully burning his salary check. In other words, "greed" simply means that you are trying to relieve the nature given scarcity that man was born with. Greed will continue until the Garden of Eden arrives, when everything is superabundant, and we don't have to worry about economics at all. We haven't of course reached that point yet; we haven't reached the point where everybody is burning his salary increases, or salary checks in general."
— Murray N. Rothbard

"The history of all hitherto existing society is the history of class struggles.

Freeman and slave, patrician and plebeian, lord and serf, guildmaster and journeyman, in a word, oppressor and oppressed, stood in constant opposition to one another, carried on an uninterrupted, now hidden, now open fight, that each time ended, either in the revolutionary reconstitution of society at large, or in the common ruin of the contending classes."

— Karl Marx, The Communist Manifesto

"How do you tell a Communist? Well, it's someone who reads Marx and Lenin. And how do you tell an anti-Communist? It's someone who understands Marx and Lenin."

— Ronald Reagan

"The ideal subject of totalitarian rule is not the convinced Nazi or the convinced Communist, but people for whom the distinction between fact and fiction (i.e., the reality of experience) and the distinction between true and false (i.e., the standards of thought) no longer exist."

— **Hannah Arendt, The Origins of Totalitarianism**

"When I give food to the poor, they call me a saint. When I ask why the poor have no food, they call me a communist."

— Dom Helder Camara, Dom Helder Camara: Essential Writings

Pick a leader who will keep jobs in your country by offering companies incentives to hire only within their borders, not one who allows corporations to outsource jobs for cheaper labor when there is a national employment crisis. Choose a leader who will invest in building bridges, not walls. Books, not weapons. Morality, not corruption. Intellectualism and wisdom, not ignorance. Stability, not fear and terror. Peace, not chaos. Love, not hate.

Convergence, not segregation. Tolerance, not discrimination. Fairness, not hypocrisy. Substance, not superficiality. Character, not immaturity. Transparency, not secrecy. Justice, not lawlessness. Environmental improvement and preservation, not destruction. Truth, not lies."

― Suzy Kassem, Rise Up and Salute the Sun: The Writings of Suzy Kassem

"I've never understood America," said the king.
"Neither do we, sir. You might say we have two governments, kind of overlapping. First we have the elected government. It's Democratic or Republican, doesn't make much difference, and then there's corporation government."
"They get along together, these governments?"
"Sometimes," said Tod. "I don't understand it myself. You see, the elected government pretends to be democratic, and actually it is autocratic. The corporation governments pretend to be autocratic and they're all the time accusing the others of socialism. They hate socialism."
"So I have heard," said Pippin.
"Well, here's the funny thing, sir. You take a big corporation in America, say like General Motors or Du Pont or U.S. Steel. The thing they're most afraid of is socialism, and at the same time they themselves are socialist states."
The king sat bolt upright. "Please?" he said.
"Well, just look at it, sir. They've got medical care for employees and their families and accident insurance and retirement pensions, paid vacations -- even vacation places -- and they're beginning to get guaranteed pay over the year. The employees have representation in pretty nearly everything, even the color they

paint the factories. As a matter of fact, they've got socialism that makes the USSR look silly."

— John Steinbeck, The Short Reign of Pippin IV

Notes, questions, epiphanies, ideas, and connections:

Chapter 6: Media Literacy and Propaganda

Once you understand that politics is the struggle for power in society, it is also important to see how power uses information and misinformation in order to achieve their aims. Understanding the basics of media literacy is critical to both the search for truth, but also how media affects our lives in both a positive and negative way. My primary goal is to show how to see through media tricks, but one can also use these lessons as a business person in order to sell more products, and increase profits.

In an era of information overload and rapid dissemination of ideas, the study of propaganda and media literacy has never been more vital. Propaganda, with its persuasive techniques and manipulation of information, has the power to shape public opinion, influence decision-making, and even manipulate entire societies. By delving into the study of propaganda, we develop a critical lens to navigate the complex media landscape, distinguishing between fact and fiction, identifying biases, and understanding the motives behind persuasive messaging. Media literacy, on the other hand, equips us with the tools to analyze and evaluate the messages conveyed through various media channels, including traditional and digital platforms. It enables us to become discerning consumers of information, adept at recognizing the strategies employed to influence our beliefs, values, and behaviors. The study of propaganda and media literacy empowers us to question, challenge, and think independently, fostering a more informed and responsible citizenry capable of navigating the complexities of a media-saturated world (Open AI).

"One of the saddest lessons of history is this: If we've been bamboozled long enough, we tend to reject any evidence of the bamboozle. We're no longer interested in finding out the truth. The bamboozle has captured us. It's simply too painful to acknowledge, even to ourselves, that we've been taken. Once you give a charlatan power over you, you almost never get it back."

― Carl Sagan, The Demon-Haunted World: Science as a Candle in the Dark

"Any sufficiently advanced technology is indistinguishable from magic."
― Arthur C. Clarke, Profiles of the Future: An Inquiry into the Limits of the Possible

"You never change things by fighting the existing reality.
To change something, build a new model that makes the existing model obsolete."
― Buckminster Fuller

"Before you become too entranced with gorgeous gadgets and mesmerizing video displays, let me remind you that information is not knowledge, knowledge is not wisdom, and wisdom is not foresight. Each grows out of the other, and we need them all."
― Arthur C. Clarke

The test of the machine is the satisfaction it gives you. There isn't any other test. If the machine produces tranquility it's right. If it disturbs you it's wrong until either the machine or your mind is changed."

— Robert M. Pirsig, Zen and the Art of Motorcycle Maintenance: An Inquiry Into Values

"We can't jump off bridges anymore because our iPhones will get ruined. We can't take skinny dips in the ocean because there's no service on the beach and adventures aren't real unless they're on Instagram. Technology has doomed the spontaneity of adventure and we're helping destroy it every time we Google, check-in, and hashtag."
— Jeremy Glass

"We refuse to turn off our computers, turn off our phone, log off Facebook, and just sit in silence, because in those moments we might actually have to face up to who we really are."
— Jefferson Bethke, Jesus Greater Than Religion

"The real problem of humanity is the following: We have Paleolithic emotions, medieval institutions and godlike technology. And it is terrifically dangerous, and it is now approaching a point of crisis overall."
— Edward O. Wilson

"As cities grow and technology takes over the world, belief and imagination fade away and so do we."
— Julie Kagawa, The Iron King

"The production of too many useful things results in too many useless people."
— Karl Marx

"Science and technology multiply around us. To an increasing extent they dictate the languages in which we speak and think. Either we use those languages, or we remain mute." J.G. Ballard

"In the age of technology there is constant access to vast amounts of information. The basket overflows; people get overwhelmed; the eye of the storm is not so much what goes on in the world, it is the confusion of how to think, feel, digest, and react to what goes on."
— Criss Jami, Venus in Arms

To understand propaganda, here are ten key terms that are essential to its study and analysis:

Propaganda: Information or material disseminated with the intention to influence attitudes, beliefs, or actions of a target audience. Propaganda often employs persuasive techniques and appeals to emotions, rather than presenting objective or balanced information.

Mass Media / Corporate Media

Independent media

What are the pros and cons of each?

Social media

Democratization

Algorithm

Big Data

Psychogenic profiling

Ideological bubble / silo

Echo chamber

Persuasion: The act of convincing or influencing others to adopt a particular belief, opinion, or behavior. Persuasion techniques are used in propaganda to shape public opinion and gain support for a specific cause or agenda.

Manipulation: The deliberate and deceptive control or influence of people's thoughts, feelings, or actions for personal or political gain. Propaganda often involves manipulation tactics, such as selective presentation of facts or emotional manipulation.

Loaded Language: The use of emotionally charged or biased words and phrases designed to evoke a strong response in the audience. Loaded language is commonly employed in propaganda to create a favorable or unfavorable perception of a particular idea or group.

Denotative language

Connotative language

Stereotyping: Generalized and oversimplified representations or images of a particular group, often based on prejudices or preconceived notions. Stereotyping is used in propaganda to promote a specific worldview or to demonize or dehumanize an opposing group.

Disinformation: False or misleading information deliberately spread to deceive or manipulate others. Disinformation is a key element of propaganda, aiming to distort reality, undermine trust in institutions, or promote a specific narrative.

Media Manipulation: The deliberate control or distortion of information and narratives by those in power or with specific agendas. Media manipulation can involve censorship, biased reporting, or the use of propaganda techniques to shape public opinion.

Repetition: The consistent and repeated use of messages, slogans, or images to reinforce specific ideas or beliefs. Repetition is a powerful technique in propaganda as it helps to create familiarity, reinforce narratives, and shape public memory.

Censorship: The suppression or control of information, ideas, or media content to prevent the dissemination of certain perspectives or to promote a particular narrative. Censorship is used in propaganda to control the flow of information and restrict access to alternative viewpoints.

Target Audience: The specific group or demographic that propaganda aims to influence. Propaganda campaigns are designed with a target audience in mind, tailoring messages and techniques to appeal to their beliefs, values, and interests.

Psychological Warfare: The use of psychological tactics, such as propaganda, manipulation, and intimidation, to undermine the morale, beliefs, or decision-making processes of an opponent. Psychological warfare aims to gain an advantage in conflicts or disputes.

The History of Memes and Their Use as Political Propaganda

The term "meme" was first introduced by the evolutionary biologist Richard Dawkins in his 1976 book, "The Selfish Gene." Dawkins coined the term to describe an idea, behavior, or style that spreads from person to person within a culture. Over time, with the advent of the internet and the ubiquity of social media, the word "meme" has become synonymous with virally transmitted cultural symbols or social ideas, often represented in image or video format. Memes have evolved into a potent tool for communication, often humorous but increasingly used for various other purposes including political propaganda.

Evolution of Memes

The early internet memes were rudimentary, largely circulated through email chains or primitive websites. Examples include the Dancing Baby and "All Your Base Are Belong To Us." As the internet evolved, so did the complexity and reach of memes. Websites like 4chan, Reddit, and later, social media platforms such as Twitter, Instagram, and Facebook played a pivotal role in the widespread distribution of memes.

Memes as Political Propaganda

The power of memes to influence public opinion became evident when they began to be weaponized for political purposes. The simplicity and humor typically associated with memes makes them easily digestible and shareable, characteristics that make them ideal for conveying political messages to vast audiences.

One of the earliest instances of memes being used for political propaganda on a large scale was during the 2008 U.S. presidential election. Barack Obama's "Hope" poster, designed by artist Shepard Fairey, became an iconic representation of the candidate's campaign. The image was widely shared, modified, and memed in countless ways.

Fast forward to the 2016 U.S. presidential election, memes played an even more pronounced role. The "Pepe the Frog" meme, originally a neutral character from a comic series, was co-opted and transformed into various political avatars, most notably associated with the alt-right movement. Conversely, memes mocking Donald Trump, such as "Tiny Hands Trump" or those juxtaposing him with Bernie Sanders, were also rampant.

Outside the U.S., during the Brexit campaign in 2016, memes played a significant role in shaping public perceptions and opinions. Pro-Brexit memes highlighting issues like immigration and EU bureaucracy went viral, while anti-Brexit memes lampooning figures like Nigel Farage or focusing on potential economic fallout also found their audiences.

Implications and Controversies

While memes can be a democratic tool allowing many voices to be heard, they also have the potential for misuse. In recent years, state actors and organized troll farms have been found to use memes to spread disinformation and sway elections. The investigation into Russian interference in the 2016 U.S. presidential election, for instance, uncovered numerous meme-based ads on Facebook aimed at deepening societal divisions.

Furthermore, the reductive nature of memes – boiling down complex political issues into bite-sized, often overly simplistic representations – can contribute to polarized public debates where nuance is lost.

Memes have transformed from harmless internet jokes to powerful tools of communication and persuasion. As with many technological advancements, they have both their benefits and drawbacks. When wielded with care and integrity, memes can be a means of engaging the masses in political discourse. However, in the hands of malicious actors, they can become tools of disinformation and division. As the digital age progresses, the importance of media literacy cannot be overstated, and understanding the power and potential pitfalls of memes is an essential part of this literacy (Open AI).

Memes and the Creation of Meaning for Specific Audiences

Memes, as pieces of cultural information that are transmitted virally, are essentially a form of shorthand communication. They work by encapsulating complex ideas, emotions, and narratives into easily digestible and shareable units. These units then find resonance with specific audiences based on shared cultural, ideological, or emotional values.

1. Utilizing Shared Cultural Context:

The efficacy of a meme largely depends on the audience's familiarity with its underlying context. For instance, a meme referencing a scene from a popular television show will carry meaning primarily for those who have seen that show. In politics, memes that refer to specific speeches, events, or political gaffes rely on the audience's prior knowledge to make sense.

2. Amplifying Emotional Resonance:

Memes often appeal to emotions, be it humor, anger, pride, or nostalgia. A meme that evokes a strong emotional response is more likely to be shared. In politics, memes can be employed to elicit feelings of hope, indignation, or ridicule, ensuring that the audience remains engaged or mobilized around a specific issue or candidate.

3. Reinforcing Group Identity:

Memes can foster a sense of belonging by highlighting in-group markers and differentiating from out-groups. Political memes often play on these dynamics, emphasizing the shared beliefs of one group while contrasting them with the perceived shortcomings of opposing groups.

Implications for Politics

1. Engagement and Mobilization:
The ease of sharing memes means they can rapidly reach large audiences. Memes that resonate emotionally or ideologically with voters can serve as a rallying cry, encouraging political activism, and participation. For example, during various protest movements globally, memes have played a significant role in galvanizing public support.

2. Simplification and Reductionism:
The inherent brevity of memes can lead to oversimplification. Complex political issues are distilled into a single image or

catchphrase, which might not capture the full nuance of the subject. This can result in a public discourse that is more polarized and less informed.

3. Disinformation and Propaganda:
Given their viral nature, memes can be a potent tool for spreading disinformation. If a misleading or entirely false meme resonates with an audience's pre-existing beliefs or biases, it can spread rapidly, shaping perceptions regardless of its veracity.

4. Shaping Narratives:
Memes play a significant role in framing political narratives. A single viral meme can determine how an event is perceived by the public. For instance, during debates, a candidate's minor slip-up turned into a meme can overshadow their substantial policy discussions.

5. Deepening Polarization:
Memes that play to in-group dynamics can exacerbate divisions in the political landscape. By repeatedly emphasizing differences and mocking or vilifying opposing groups, memes can create an "us vs. them" mentality, reducing opportunities for meaningful dialogue.

Conclusion

Memes, due to their viral nature and appeal to emotion and shared cultural contexts, are a formidable force in shaping political perceptions and narratives. Their influence on modern political discourse cannot be understated. While they hold the promise of engaging and mobilizing audiences, they also bear the risks of deepening divisions and spreading misinformation. As with all forms of media, a critical and discerning approach to political memes is essential for a healthy democratic process (Open AI).

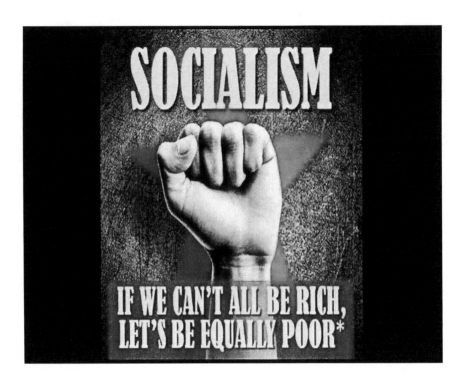

SOCIALISM

Socialism is taxpayer funds being used collectively to benefit society as a whole, despite income, contribution, or ability.

Medicare	Free Lunch Program
Social Security	SNAP
Public Schools	FDA
The Military/Defense	Unemployment Insurance
Highways/Roads	OSHA
Public Libraries	USDA
Fire Department	National Weather Service
Police	CDC
Student Loans & Grants	Sewer System
Farm Subsidies	Medicaid
CIA & FBI	Jail/Prison System
Polio Vaccine	Court System
EPA	Health Care 9/11 Workers
Museums	Disability Insurance
Public Parks	Town/State Run Beaches
VA	State Construction
GI Bill	State Snow Removal
Hoover Dam	Public Street Lighting
Bridges	and more -DailyKos

Memes and stereotypes:

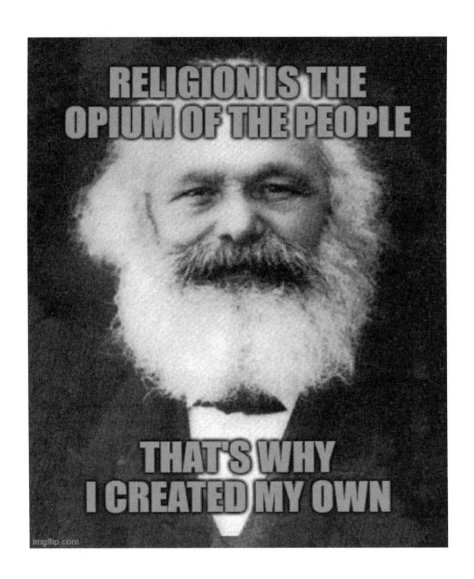

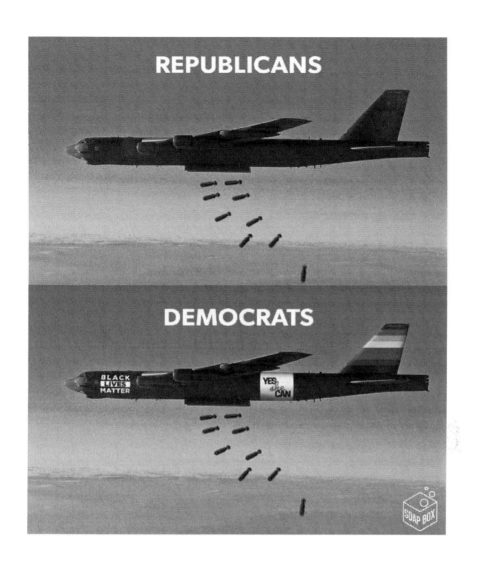

Memes are a chunk of cultural information that spreads within a culture. They are also short and sometimes humorous pictures with captions on them or viral videos or sayings.

Because they are short, they frequently rely on stereotyping in order to function.

A stereotype is a preconceived notion that all people, places or things are alike.

A stereotype is also a way of "Othering."

Many peer groups engage in othering. Othering is also born of collective and individual identity.

Dominant culture / ideology – the values of the group with the most power in society.

Master narrative—the narrative told by the dominant social group in order to maintain, justify or expand power.

Counter-narrative—a narrative that seeks to overthrow the dominant social group in order to become the master narrative.

Dialectical narrative-a narrative that seeks to integrate the master and counter narrative as well as other narratives in order to understand it.

Cultural stereotype—refers to the meaning a person, place or idea that a specific culture places upon something, and whether or not it has positive or negative
connotations.

Denotation: the dictionary definition of a word.

Connotation: the ideas we associate closely with a word, whether positive, negative or sexual in nature.

Think of "Obamacare, " for example, that is a word that has positive and negative connotations depending on whether or not you are a fan of Obama.

Othering is the process of seeing somebody as outside the dominant group, and therefore inferior.

Racism, classism, sexism, etc. are all kinds of Othering, but you can also other somebody for their looks, athletic ability, intelligence, age, height, etc.

Othering can be put on a continuum in terms of its proclivity to do harm toward others.

There can be different variables for why somebody is othered, such as race, class, and gender, social group, religion, etc. Looking at these variables is called intersectionality.

Other-somebody outside a dominant cultural group.

This meme shows Bernie Sanders at a podium speaking forcefully. The caption reads, "We can pay for Education with Pixie Dust." This reinforces the stereotype that Bernie is a pie in the sky dreamer, and consequently that everyone who votes for socialist policies is as well." It implies that capitalists are social Darwinists are the ones who live in the real world. It wants you to be against socialist policies, such as education.

The meme shows president Trump throwing up his arms with a confused look on his face. The caption reads, "I keep trying to call the president of Puerto Rico, but the line is always busy." It reinforces the stereotype that Trump is unintelligent by showing his ignorance to the fact that the reason the line might be busy is that Puerto Rico is a legal territory of the U.S. and he would therefore be the president. It implies that the reason why Trump has not been able to help Puerto Rico is due to his lack of understanding of his role. It is, therefore, arguing for the removal of Trump for somebody who might understand the world better.

The meme shows Willy Wonka staring at Charlie with the face that he knows something Charlie doesn't. The caption reads, "That was a pretty funny political meme you shared with us. Thanks for your help with fixing America." The stereotype here is Willy Wonka who knows it all, and speaking ironically about something he knows that Charlie or in this case (we) don't. And that is how little funny memes are helpful in "fixing" the problems of America. It is implying that posting political memes are a waste of time, and that real change probably comes from doing more such as voting, etc.

Questions:

1) What happens when we run across a meme and don't understand the cultural
references and stereotypes?

2) How do our own values and beliefs play into our reading of a meme?

3) How do we understand a meme that is for an audience with a different frame?

This might also be called a meta-meme or a meme about memes.

Find 3 political memes; at least one liberal and one conservative.

Briefly describe the picture, and the caption.

Tell me what stereotypes the meme relies on about people, places, things or ideas.

Tell me what the meme is arguing for, and against.

Tell me if you could upgrade the meme, and how?
This means make the argument more clear vs. change the argument.

Another concept that is very important to help understand how modern politics is sold to people is "branding":

Definition: Branding, in its essence, is the process of creating a unique image, name, or symbol that identifies and differentiates a product or entity from its competitors in the eyes of the consumer. It involves consistent messaging, imagery, and positioning to establish a distinct identity.

Branding in Politics:

Personal Brand of a Politician: Just like companies, politicians also develop a brand around their persona. This includes their style of communication, principles they stand by, their history, and any other distinctive attributes that make them recognizable. For instance, Bernie Sanders in the U.S. has branded himself around progressive policies, grassroots campaigns, and consistency in his political positions over decades.

Party Branding: Political parties establish branding through logos, slogans, and platforms. The Democratic donkey and the Republican elephant in the U.S. are symbolic brand identifiers. Parties also consistently reinforce their brand through policy stances (e.g., fiscal conservatism for Republicans or social progressivism for Democrats).

Campaign Themes and Slogans: A memorable campaign slogan can reinforce a political brand. "Hope and Change" became synonymous with Barack Obama's 2008 campaign, while "Make America Great Again" did the same for Donald Trump's 2016 campaign.

Visual Branding: Politicians and political movements often utilize specific colors, logos, and visual motifs in their campaigns. These visual cues help make their messages more memorable and create a sense of unity among supporters.

Issue-based Branding: Politicians may brand themselves based on specific issues they champion. For instance, a politician might brand themselves as a "champion of the environment" or a "defender of the Second Amendment."

Rebranding: Just as companies might rebrand when their image becomes outdated or tarnished, politicians also sometimes attempt to rebrand themselves, especially after scandals, policy failures, or shifts in public opinion.

Digital Branding: In the age of social media, politicians use platforms like Twitter, Facebook, and Instagram to shape their brands. The manner in which they engage with followers, the issues they highlight, and the imagery they use all contribute to their digital brand identity.

Implications of Branding in Politics:

Branding in politics can be a double-edged sword. On the one hand, a strong brand can create a dedicated base of supporters, simplify complex issues for voters, and make a politician or party more recognizable. On the other hand, if a political brand is perceived as inauthentic or becomes associated with negative events or policies, it can be challenging to change those perceptions.

Ultimately, branding in politics, as in the commercial world, is about creating an emotional connection and a sense of trust with the audience. Successful politicians often manage to do this by effectively communicating their values, vision, and personality through a consistent brand identity.

Focus groups

Think tanks

Public Relations (PR)

Media Bias: The systematic favoritism or prejudice in the way news organizations or journalists present information, stories, or opinions. Media bias can manifest in various forms, such as partisan bias, ideological bias, or corporate bias.

Confirmation Bias: The tendency of individuals to seek or interpret information in a way that confirms their existing beliefs or preconceived notions. Confirmation bias can affect both media producers and consumers, leading to the selection or interpretation of news that aligns with personal biases.

Gatekeeping: The process by which media organizations select, filter, and control the flow of information to the public. Gatekeeping decisions, such as story selection, source inclusion, or framing, can introduce bias based on editorial judgment or organizational interests.

Agenda Setting: The power of the media to influence public opinion and shape the salience and importance of certain issues or topics. Media outlets can prioritize specific stories or perspectives, which can result in biased coverage by emphasizing particular narratives while downplaying others.

Framing: The presentation or context in which news stories or issues are portrayed, shaping how audiences interpret or understand them. Framing choices, such as language, imagery, or focus, can introduce bias by emphasizing certain aspects or promoting particular interpretations.

Selective Reporting: The intentional or unintentional omission or underrepresentation of certain news stories or perspectives. Selective reporting can create a skewed perception of events and issues, leading to bias through incomplete or unbalanced coverage.

Sensationalism: The practice of emphasizing dramatic, shocking, or emotionally charged aspects of news stories to attract attention and increase audience engagement. Sensationalism can introduce bias by prioritizing sensational or controversial elements over factual and nuanced reporting.

Fact-Checking: The process of verifying and evaluating the accuracy and reliability of information presented in news stories. Fact-checking plays a crucial role in identifying and correcting biased or misleading reporting, promoting transparency and accountability in the media.

Understanding media bias involves critically evaluating the sources, methods, and motivations behind news reporting. Being aware of these terms can help individuals navigate the media landscape and develop a more discerning and informed approach to consuming news.

Objectivity: The principle of presenting information without bias or personal opinion. Media outlets strive for objectivity in their reporting, but achieving complete objectivity can be challenging due to inherent biases and subjective judgments.

Balance: The practice of presenting multiple perspectives or viewpoints on a particular issue to provide a fair and comprehensive understanding. Balancing reporting can help mitigate bias by ensuring diverse voices and opinions are represented.

Spin: The deliberate manipulation or framing of information to present it in a favorable or negative light. Spin often involves selective emphasis, strategic wording, or the omission of certain details to shape public perception.

Source Bias: Bias that arises from the bias or agenda of the sources used in news reporting. Journalists rely on sources for information, and if those sources have inherent biases or motivations, it can influence the objectivity of the reporting.

Editorializing: The inclusion of personal opinions or subjective commentary in news reporting. Editorializing blurs the line between factual reporting and opinion, potentially introducing bias into the coverage.

Media Ownership: The control and ownership of media outlets by individuals, corporations, or organizations. Media ownership can influence the editorial stance and content produced, potentially leading to bias based on the interests or ideologies of the owners.

Media Literacy: The ability to critically analyze and evaluate media messages, sources, and biases. Media literacy empowers individuals to recognize and navigate media bias, enabling them to make more informed judgments about the information they consume.

Ethical Journalism: The practice of adhering to professional and ethical standards in reporting, which includes accuracy, fairness, and transparency. Ethical journalism seeks to minimize bias and promote responsible and accountable reporting.

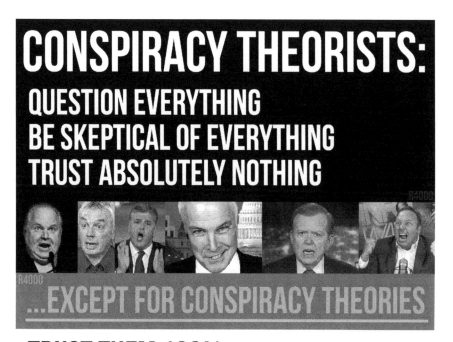

Chapter 7: Conspiracy theories and cults

It is also impossible to talk about politics and argumentation without talking a little bit about the effect of conspiracy theories on American politics.

History of Conspiracy Thinking in the United States

Conspiracy thinking has deep roots in American history, and the country's founding was, in many ways, informed by concerns about secretive plots. Over the years, numerous conspiracy theories have gained traction, affecting public perception and, at times, policy. The advent of the internet has amplified the spread of such theories.

Pre-20th Century:

The Salem Witch Trials (1692-1693): Fears of witchcraft and the devil led to a widespread belief that certain individuals were conspiring against the Puritan community. This resulted in the execution of twenty people, most of them women.

Anti-Masonic Movement (1820s-1830s): Concerns about the secretive nature of the Freemasons led to suspicions that they were plotting to overthrow the republic. This paranoia even spawned the Anti-Masonic Party, which participated in the presidential elections.

20th Century:

Red Scare (1919-1920 and 1950s): Fears of communist infiltration led to widespread suspicions, resulting in events such as the

Hollywood blacklist and the notorious investigations by Senator Joseph McCarthy.

JFK Assassination (1963): The assassination of President John F. Kennedy spurred numerous conspiracy theories. These ranged from suspicions about the CIA, to the mafia, to foreign governments.

Moon Landing (1969): Despite substantial evidence, some believed that the Apollo moon landing was staged by the U.S. government to claim victory in the space race against the Soviet Union.

The Internet Era:

The rise of the internet, and especially platforms like YouTube, Facebook, and various forums, has facilitated the rapid dissemination of conspiracy theories. The decentralized nature of the internet allows for echo chambers, where individuals are rarely exposed to contradicting viewpoints.

9/11 Attacks: The tragedy of September 11th gave rise to numerous conspiracy theories, such as controlled demolitions or the U.S. government's prior knowledge of the attacks. Internet forums and websites dedicated to these theories proliferated.

Birther Conspiracy: This theory falsely claimed that President Barack Obama wasn't born in the U.S. It gained significant traction online and was even propagated by prominent figures, including Donald Trump before his presidency.

QAnon: Originating from anonymous message boards, this unfounded conspiracy theory claims that a secret cabal of elites is involved in various crimes, and that President Trump was leading a fight against them. This theory has had real-world implications, with believers engaging in acts of violence or making political decisions based on its tenets.

Reasons for the Rise in Conspiracy Thinking with the Internet:

Access to Information: While the internet democratized access to information, it also allowed for the rapid spread of misinformation.

Echo Chambers: Algorithms of social media platforms often show users content similar to what they've previously engaged with, reinforcing existing beliefs and insulating them from contradictory information.

Anonymity: The anonymous nature of many online platforms allows users to spread theories without accountability.

Legitimization: Online, conspiracy theories can be presented with a veneer of credibility, using out-of-context evidence, official-sounding language, or manipulated images and videos.

Global Reach: Before the internet, conspiracy theories often remained localized. The internet allows for their rapid global dissemination.

Conclusion:

Conspiracy thinking in the U.S. is not new, but the internet has transformed the way these theories spread and gain traction. The implications of this are profound, influencing everything from public health (e.g., vaccine hesitancy) to political elections. The challenge moving forward is fostering digital literacy and critical thinking in an era of information overload.

While many conspiracy theories are unfounded and lack evidence, there have been instances in history where suspicions or "conspiracies" were later proven to be based on factual events. Some notable examples include:

Operation Northwoods (1960s): This was a proposed plan by the U.S. Department of Defense to stage acts of terrorism on American soil or against American interests. These acts would be blamed on Cuba to justify military intervention in the country. The operation was never approved or carried out, but documents related to the proposal were declassified in the 1990s.

The Tuskegee Syphilis Study (1932-1972): For four decades, the U.S. Public Health Service conducted an unethical clinical study on Black men in Tuskegee, Alabama. These men had syphilis and were deceived by researchers, who withheld adequate treatment from them to study the progression of the disease. The truth came out in the 1970s, leading to significant changes in ethical guidelines for research.

COINTELPRO (1956-1971): This was a covert FBI program designed to surveil, infiltrate, and disrupt American political organizations. While its targets spanned a broad range of groups, it notoriously targeted civil rights organizations and leaders, including Dr. Martin Luther King Jr. Documents revealing the extent of COINTELPRO were leaked, and further details emerged during Senate investigations in the 1970s.

Operation Mockingbird (1950s-1970s): Initiated by the CIA, this operation aimed to influence media and news outlets during the

Cold War. While the exact extent of the CIA's control over news is debated, it's confirmed that the agency had relationships with journalists and news executives, aiming to sway public opinion and gather information.

The Iran-Contra Affair (1980s): Members of the Reagan administration secretly facilitated the sale of arms to Iran, which was under an arms embargo. The proceeds from these sales were then covertly funneled to Contra rebels fighting the Sandinista government in Nicaragua. The scandal became public in 1986.

Operation CHAOS (1967-1973): Another CIA operation, this one aimed to monitor the activities of left-wing activists and organizations during the 1960s and 70s. It was intended to uncover any foreign influences behind the anti-Vietnam War movement. The program involved a significant amount of domestic surveillance, raising questions about its legality.

MKUltra (1950s-1970s): A clandestine CIA operation focused on researching mind control and chemical interrogation methods. The program involved administering LSD and other drugs to unwitting subjects, among other experiments. Its existence and details were exposed in the 1970s through investigative journalism and congressional investigations.

It's important to differentiate between conspiracy theories and actual conspiracies. The former are often rooted in speculation and lack concrete evidence, while the latter have been proven or substantiated through credible sources, investigations, or declassified documents.

The "Baader-Meinhof phenomenon" (not hypothesis) is also commonly referred to as "frequency illusion." The name "Baader-Meinhof" can be misleading, as it's also the name of a notorious German terrorist group from the 1970s. The term's association with the frequency illusion is more anecdotal than systematic.

The Baader-Meinhof phenomenon describes the experience when someone learns or notices something new, like a word or a concept, and then starts to recognize it everywhere in a short span of time. It feels like that thing has suddenly increased in frequency, when in reality it's just that the person has become more aware of it.

The phenomenon can be broken down into two cognitive biases:

Selective Attention Bias: Once a new word, idea, or concept is learned, our brains unconsciously look for it everywhere, making it more "visible" to us.

Confirmation Bias: Every time we recognize this new thing, our brain celebrates it as a confirmation or proof of its increased frequency, further solidifying the illusion.

While the Baader-Meinhof phenomenon is an interesting cognitive quirk, it's a good reminder of how our perceptions can be influenced and aren't always an accurate representation of reality.

Conspiracy Theory: A belief or explanation suggesting that events or situations are the result of a covert, often sinister, plot by a group or organization, rather than arising from transparent or overt causes.

Confirmation Bias: The tendency to search for, interpret, and remember information in a way that confirms one's preexisting beliefs.

Cognitive Dissonance: Psychological discomfort that arises from holding two or more conflicting beliefs or attitudes at the same time. Some people might adopt conspiracy theories to alleviate such discomfort.

Cherry Picking: Selecting only certain pieces of information to support a viewpoint while ignoring contradictory evidence.

Anomaly Hunting: Actively searching for anomalies or peculiarities in data or events, often without regard to the broader context, to support a conspiratorial claim.

Pareidolia: The human tendency to recognize patterns, like faces or meaningful symbols, in random or unrelated data.

Proportionality Bias: The inclination to believe that significant events must have significant causes. For example, believing a vast conspiracy led to an impactful event rather than a simpler explanation.

Overactive Agency Detection: The tendency to attribute events to deliberate actions rather than chance, accident, or natural causes.

Galileo Gambit: A rhetorical strategy where one argues that because their ideas are ridiculed or persecuted, they must be correct, drawing an analogy to Galileo Galilei's persecution.

In-group vs. Out-group: Social psychology terms related to defining one's identity group in opposition to others. Conspiracy theories can strengthen in-group cohesion by painting out-groups as threats.

Epistemic Closure: The refusal to allow new information to challenge or modify one's existing beliefs. This can lead to a rigid worldview where conspiracy theories go unchallenged.

Post-truth: Relating to or denoting circumstances in which emotional or belief-driven opinions have more influence on public opinion than objective facts.

False Flag Operation: A covert operation designed to deceive by making it appear as though it was carried out by another entity. Conspiracy theories often suggest events were "false flag" operations.

Understanding these terms provides a foundational vocabulary to delve deeper into the psychology and sociology of conspiracy theories and those who endorse them.

Confirmation Loop: This refers to the continuous cycle where a belief leads individuals to seek out and identify new evidence supporting that belief, which in turn strengthens the original belief.

Cui Bono: A Latin term meaning "who benefits?" Conspiracists frequently use this line of reasoning, suggesting that if someone benefits from an event, they must have orchestrated it.

Compartmentalization: In the context of conspiracy theories, this term suggests that information or plans are divided among a limited number of individuals, so that even people within the group don't have a complete picture, making the conspiracy difficult to expose.

Shill: An individual who discredits or pretends to be part of the conspiracy community but is believed to be deceiving the group. Accusations of being a "shill" can be used to dismiss those who challenge or debunk conspiracy theories.

Occam's Razor: A principle suggesting that the simplest explanation (the one making the fewest assumptions) is most likely the correct one. While not specific to conspiracy theories, it's frequently cited in discussions to counter overly complex conspiratorial explanations.

Controlled Opposition: The belief that some figures or groups who appear to be against a conspiracy or the establishment are secretly controlled by it. This idea suggests that these figures or groups exist to give the appearance of genuine dissent.

Just in case somebody wants to bring up anti-semitic arguments about Jewish bankers, here are some non-Jewish members of Blackrock's board, a virtual rainbow of friendly financiers:
William F. Ford
Bader Mohammed Al Sa'ad
Pamela Daley
Fabrezio Freda
Peggy Johnson
Cheryl Mills
Gordon Nixon
Chuck Robbins
Mark Wilson

Amir Nasser
Murry S. Gerben
Key Terms to understanding cult-like behavior:

Cult:

Understanding cult-like behavior involves recognizing certain psychological, social, and organizational patterns. Here are ten essential terms that can help elucidate the dynamics of cults and their operations:

Charismatic Leadership: Refers to the magnetic charm and appeal of certain leaders, often the central figure in cults. Followers often believe in the infallibility or divine guidance of such leaders.

Brainwashing (or Thought Reform): A process by which individuals are subjected to systematic and intense persuasion techniques to change their beliefs and attitudes, often resulting in the uncritical adoption of the cult's beliefs.

Deindividuation: The loss of self-awareness and individuality, often seen in group settings. In cults, this can result in members conforming to group norms and behaviors without questioning.

Isolation: Many cults isolate their members from family, friends, and the broader society to control their information flow, environment, and reduce dissenting views.

Love Bombing: A manipulation technique where new members are showered with affection, attention, and kindness to make them feel special and to foster loyalty to the group.

Us vs. Them Mentality: Cults often foster a worldview where they are the enlightened or chosen ones, while outsiders are seen as misguided, evil, or a threat.

Groupthink: A phenomenon where the desire for harmony and conformity in a group results in an incorrect or deviant decision-making outcome. Members suppress dissenting viewpoints, isolate themselves from outside influences, and believe in the inherent morality of the group.

Milieu Control: Controlling all communication within an environment, including interpersonal communication. This ensures that the group's narrative is accepted without challenge.

Exit Costs: High emotional, social, or financial costs associated with leaving the group. This could include shunning, threats, fear of retribution, or losing one's salvation or purpose.

Doomsday Scenarios: Many cults hold beliefs about apocalyptic events or prophesied calamities, suggesting that only the faithful (or members of the cult) will survive or be saved.

Understanding these terms provides a foundational vocabulary to delve into the psychology and dynamics of cults and their members. Remember that not all groups labeled as "cults" by outsiders necessarily exhibit all of these characteristics.

Chapter 8: Arguments, fallacies, and reason

Key terms to understanding verbal arguments.

What is an argument?

An argument is a statement or claim that also has reasoning.

The statement "the Oregon Ducks are the best" is not an argument per se; it is a statement until you give some reasoning or a "because," such as in the statement: The Oregon Ducks are the best **because** they won the National Championship."

Now we have an argument. There is a statement or claim AND reasoning. The next step to understanding an argument is to know how an argument might be picked apart. The first and most important way is through the definition of key terms. In the above example the term "best" is vague and needs to be clarified to be argued. What do you mean by best? Is it whoever won the National Championship? or whoever had the toughest schedule? Or whoever had the best win-loss record? Or some combination of these variables? Frequently there are arguments that go on in a hideously dichotomous fashion because there is no set of agreement as to what one means by a given term. These arguments are called arguing over "semantics" or the meaning of a word, and it is only after an agreement of the key terms that one can even proceed to the next step, which is finding support and evidence.

Let us say, for example, we agree that the best team is the one with the best win-loss record for the season. Then we can proceed by looking up a credible source and finding out who is correct. In this case the NCAA website is probably a credible source since it is in charge of regulating college sports. So I went to their website and discovered that Oregon had a 10-1 win-loss record and the next best team was 10 to 2. At this point the argument should be over, hands shaking, and the participants move on. The facts are in and they clearly show Oregon with the best win loss record.

This is the ideal case scenario for a simple argument with a simple answer that one could look up. Now, let's imagine that the person we are arguing with is caught in a power struggle and wants to keep dichotomously thinking so as not to "lose" the argument no matter what.

Here are first basic strategies that will probably be employed:

The first is they will redefine the issue so that the key term now means something else. This is all also called "moving the goalposts," no pun intended. They might say, for example, that what they really meant was the team with the most players recruited to the NFL or if they lose that one, then I meant the team with the coolest uniforms and on and on. This is why motive is so important to take into consideration because if the motive is power, the truth no longer matters.

Another thing they could do is find "alternative" sources, otherwise known as non-credible sources; so instead of going to the credible NCAA website, your friend instructs you to go to a website they have created called "Footballfactz.com," and since your friend has created this website with the explicit purpose of making himself right, which actually happened when I had a student whose boyfriend changed a Wikipedia entry to match his version of reality. In this case, you might find on this site that Oregon's win loss record is 7 to 3, and your friend is now right due to living in a parallel universe.

Finally, people might even conjure up a conspiracy theory peppered with half-truths that sounds so convincing that facts no longer matter. For example, the NCAA is a multi-million dollar organization known for its corruption. It's possible that officials have been bribed by Nike co-founder Phil Knight to pay the referees to make calls in favor of Oregon. Phil Knight is not only the founder and CEO of Nike, but also an alumnus of the University of Oregon therefore, even if Oregon has a better win loss record according to the NCAA, it's only because the refs are on the Nike payroll. Illuminati confirmed.

I'm not suggesting that sometimes conspiracies don't actually happen, especially when big money is involved, but the question still remains as to whether or not the person with the conspiracy theory has credible evidence to support their claim.

Let's say for example I have evidence that the number two team in the nation was also sponsored by Nike and the Phil Knight would have made more money had that team won the National Championship instead of Oregon. In addition, there are internal documents from the Nike Corporation that show that Oregon's market had already been tapped, and that this other school would be a "gold mine" if they were to become national champions.

At this point if the friend does not drop their original theory, they are probably not interested in truth or facts or research in the first place, only sticking to their point of view and "winning" the argument. Hopefully, with these examples you can see how difficult argumentation can be, even with the most clearly stated arguments and intentions.

Now we're going to look at the ways in which arguments themselves can be flawed and not follow logic; these flaws in logic are called "logical fallacies." There are too many kinds of logical fallacies for me to go over all of them. If you look them up on Wikipedia, you will find several pages full, but I think with the ones I outline here you should be able to see through almost all poor arguments that will come your way.

The Most Commonly Used Logical Fallacies with examples of illustration:

1) Semantics: Arguing over semantics means that two or more people are having a disagreement or dispute about the definition of a word or phrase, rather than the underlying issue or concept.

Here's an example: They argued over who is the best basketball player of all time, not realizing that they each had a different definition of "greatest," so that it was really a question of semantics.

2) Overgeneralization: This is a logical fallacy where a conclusion is drawn based on insufficient or incomplete evidence, and then applied to a larger group or category as if it were true for all of that category. For example, "All dogs are aggressive" after encountering one aggressive dog.

The use of absolutes statements that begin with words like "all," "every," "never," "always," etc. are clues that an overgeneralization is at work, and one might need a qualifying statement such as, "some," "most," "many," "almost," "frequently," might be needed to make the statement more correct. "All Americans are materialistic" sounds good, but if there is one American living off the land, and eating berries, then the statement is false, and so one must qualify it by saying, "Many Americans" or "Most Americans" are materialistic.

Spoiler alert: all isms, such as racism, sexism, classism, etc. are guilty of overgeneralizations.

3) False dichotomy: A false dichotomy is a logical fallacy where only two options are presented as the only possible choices, when in reality, there are more options available. It is also known as the "either/or" fallacy. For example, "You're either with us or against us" implies that there are no other options or possibilities, when in reality, there are many shades of gray between the two positions. Other examples, either your liberal or conservative, an iphone user or a samsung user, etc.

4) Faulty causality: This is a logical fallacy where one event is assumed to cause another event, without any evidence or proof to support the claim. For example, "I wore my lucky socks and won the game, so the socks caused me to win" assumes a causal relationship without any evidence. This is very similar to the idea that correlation doesn't equal causation. Just because there is a correlation between me selling more cream on days when people wear sunglasses

doesn't mean that people wearing sunglasses is what caused me to sell more ice cream.

5) Circular reasoning: This is a logical fallacy where the conclusion is used as evidence to support the premise or basically saying the same thing twice using different words. For example, "Unmarried men are single because they are bachelors."

Me: Son, you have to go to bed because it's bedtime.
Son: That's circular reasoning, Dad. Bedtime means by definition it's time to go to bed but you haven't given any reasoning as to why I have to go to bed in the first place.
Me; It's late, I had a long day.
Son: Don't try and pivot to another topic.
Me: Fine. There was a study done at Harvard that showed children who had healthy sleep patterns performed better in school, so I am saying you should go to bed so that you get enough sleep to perform well at school and have a better life."
Son: Where is this study? I need to check the sources.
Me: Get your butt to bed.
Son: Oh, I see you're going full dictator mode now.

6) Red herring: This is a logical fallacy where an irrelevant topic is introduced to divert attention from the original issue. For example, "I know I was supposed to clean my room, but what about the fact that my brother never cleans his room?" This is also called a pivot or reframe.

7) Irrelevant connection: This is when an argument begins with one thing, and ends up with another without showing how they relate. Example: marijuana leads to hard drug use, so we need to build more prisons. It's been proven

that second hand smoke can cause lung cancer, so we should support vaping in schools.

8) Strawman: This is a logical fallacy where an opponent's argument is misrepresented or exaggerated to make it easier to attack. In other words, instead of giving a real counter argument, you put up a straw man to beat up and look tough. For example, "My opponent thinks that we should just let criminals run wild in the streets and never punish them."

9) Obfuscation: This is a logical fallacy where the speaker or writer intentionally confuses or obscures the issue to make it difficult to understand. For example, somebody is wearing a swastika, and you say that it's a symbol of Nazism, and they say, "Actually, it's an ancient Tibetan symbol predating the Nazis," which may be true, but it's not the current meaning that most people have for it.

10) Whataboutism: Whataboutism is a type of logical fallacy where an individual tries to deflect criticism by pointing out the wrongdoings of others, rather than addressing the original criticism. It is an attempt to avoid taking responsibility or answering for one's own actions. For example, if someone is accused of lying, they might respond with "But what about when you lied about X?"

11) Poisoning the well: discrediting a person or organization to the point where nobody believes anything it says. Example: "For many Democrats, the well of Republicans has been poisoned, and vice versa."

12) Gish Gallop: Gish Gallop is a type of logical fallacy where someone overwhelms an opponent with a barrage of rapid-fire arguments, often relying on misdirection or falsehoods. The goal is to make it difficult or impossible for the opponent to address each point. Example: "My wife won the argument using the Gish Gallop technique."

13) Bad Analogy: A bad analogy is a type of logical fallacy where a comparison is made between two things that are not actually similar, leading to a flawed conclusion. The analogy may be based on superficial similarities, but the differences between the two things are significant enough to invalidate the comparison. For example, "People are just like chickens. They both run around all day, eating, so if it is legal to kill chickens, it should be legal to kill people."

14) The Straw man argument: This is when you deliberately misrepresent the opposing argument so that you can beat it up like a straw man.

See if you can identify at least one fallacy for each argument:

If we ban Hummers because they are bad for the environment, eventually the government will ban all cars so we should not ban Hummers.

Even though it's only the first day, I can tell this is going to be a boring course.

I drank bottled water and now I'm sick, so the water must have made me sick.

The Volkswagen Beetle is an evil car because it was originally designed by Hitler's Army.

Kanye West is a good communicator because he speaks effectively

Green Piece of strategies aren't effective because they are all dirty lazy hippies.

If you were a true American, you would support the right of people to choose whatever vehicle they want.

The level of mercury in seafood may be unsafe, but what will fishers do to support their families?

The parking attendant who gave me a ticket is as bad as Hitler

My grandfather smoked and ate poorly his whole life and he never got sick.

My roommate said her philosophy class was hard and the one I'm in is hard, so all philosophy classes must be hard.

President Jones just raised taxes and then the rate of violent crime went up. Jones is responsible for the rise in crime.

Hairspray is causing global warming because it emits harmful juices.

Part 2 logical fallacies:

A black cat crossed Babs path yesterday and sure enough she was involved in an automobile accident later that afternoon.

I'd like to hire you but your next felon and statistics show that 80% of ex-felons recidivate.

All of those movie stars are really rude. I asked Ryan Reynolds for his autograph in a restaurant in Westwood the other evening and he told me to get lost

Pit bulls are actually gentle sweet dogs my next door neighbor has one and his dog loves to romp and play with all the kids in the neighborhood

What's the big deal about the early Pioneers killing a few Indians in order to settle the West. After all, you can't make an omelet without breaking a few eggs.

We can safely conclude that there is intelligent life elsewhere in the universe because thus far no one has been able to prove that there is not.

Either you buy a large car and watch it guzzle away your paycheck or you buy a small car and take a greater risk of being injured or killed in the event of an accident.

That guy wearing a Raiders jacket and baggy pants, I'll bet he's a gang member.

There's no reason to listen to the arguments of those who oppose school prayer, for that is the argument of atheists.

Accused by his wife of cheating at cards, Ned replies, "Nothing I do ever ever pleases you. I spent all last week painting the bathroom and then you said you didn't like the colors."

Why logic doesn't solve all the world's problems:

Changing one's values and beliefs is often challenging due to a combination of psychological, cognitive, social, and even neurological factors. Here are several reasons explaining why people's values and beliefs are resistant to change:

Identity and Self-Concept: People's beliefs and values are integral to their identity. Admitting a change or that one might have been wrong about deeply held beliefs can be perceived as a threat to one's self-concept and image.

Cognitive Dissonance: This psychological theory posits that holding contradictory beliefs or values creates mental discomfort. To resolve this discomfort, individuals might reject or downplay new information that contradicts their existing beliefs rather than alter those beliefs.

Confirmation Bias: People have a tendency to seek out, interpret, and remember information in ways that affirm their pre-existing beliefs and values.

Emotional Attachment: Beliefs can be tied to powerful emotions or personal experiences. When beliefs are rooted in strong emotions, rational arguments alone might not be effective in changing them.

Sunk Cost Fallacy: If someone has invested a lot of time, energy, or resources into a particular belief or value system (e.g., being part of a religious or political group), they may find it challenging to change due to the perceived "cost" of their previous investment.

Social and Cultural Influences: Social groups, family, culture, and societal norms play a significant role in shaping and reinforcing beliefs. Going against the grain might lead to social ostracization, making it harder for individuals to change.

Fear of the Unknown: Changing a core belief or value might mean stepping into unfamiliar territory, leading to uncertainty or fear of the consequences.

Motivated Reasoning: This is a type of biased decision-making where the outcomes or conclusions are predetermined by desires or motivations, not objective analysis. If a person doesn't "want" to believe something, they'll find reasons to dismiss it.

Dunning-Kruger Effect: In some cases, individuals might overestimate their knowledge or expertise in a particular domain, leading them to dismiss contradictory information due to misplaced confidence.

Neurological Pathways: On a biological level, beliefs and habits of thinking can create well-worn neural pathways. Over time, these pathways become the brain's "default" way of thinking, making change more difficult.

Changing beliefs and values often requires more than just presenting new information or arguments. Effective strategies usually involve empathy, repeated exposure to new ideas, and creating a safe environment where individuals can explore and consider alternative perspectives without feeling threatened.

Chapter 9: Science, data, and lies

Understanding the scientific method is of utmost importance in today's world, where science plays a pivotal role in shaping our lives and driving progress. The scientific method provides a systematic and reliable framework for investigating and understanding the natural world. It is a process that involves observation, experimentation, data analysis, and drawing evidence-based conclusions. By understanding the scientific method, we gain the ability to critically evaluate scientific claims, distinguish between reliable and unreliable information, and make informed decisions based on evidence. Scientific literacy enables us to appreciate the limitations of scientific knowledge, recognize the iterative nature of scientific inquiry, and embrace the ever-evolving nature of scientific understanding. Moreover, understanding the scientific method encourages us to adopt a curious and skeptical mindset, to question assumptions, and to engage in evidence-based reasoning. Whether in the realms of healthcare, technology, environmental conservation, or policy-making, a solid understanding of the scientific method empowers individuals to engage with scientific knowledge, contribute to scientific progress, and make informed choices for a better future. (Open AI)

The layman to expert continuum

Scientific Method: The systematic approach used in scientific inquiry, involving observation, hypothesis formulation, experimentation, data collection, analysis, and conclusion drawing. The scientific method provides a structured framework for conducting scientific research.

Controlled experiment

Control group

Sample size

Observation

Hypothesis

Testing / Experimentation

Evidence

Variables

Placebo

Placebo effect

Hidden / lurking variables

Correlation doesn't mean causation

Blind experiment

Double blind experiment

Anecdotal evidence

Primary source document

Secondary source

Meta-analysis

Abstract

Statistical significance

Conflict of interest

Peer reviewed

Empiricism: The foundation of scientific knowledge based on observation, experimentation, and evidence from the physical world. Empiricism emphasizes the importance of empirical data in understanding and explaining natural phenomena.

Hypothesis: A proposed explanation or tentative answer to a scientific question. Hypotheses are formulated based on existing knowledge and are subject to testing and evaluation through experimentation.

Experiment: A controlled procedure carried out to test a hypothesis or investigate a scientific question. Experiments involve manipulating variables and observing the resulting outcomes to gather data and draw conclusions.

Theory: In scientific terms, a theory is a well-substantiated explanation of some aspect of the natural world. It is supported by a significant body of evidence and has been extensively tested and validated.

Observation: The act of carefully watching, perceiving, and recording data about natural phenomena or processes.

Observations serve as the basis for scientific inquiry and help to gather empirical evidence.

Data: Information or facts collected through observation, measurement, or experimentation. Data can be qualitative or quantitative and provide the basis for analysis and drawing conclusions.

Peer Review: The evaluation of scientific work by experts in the same field to ensure its quality, validity, and adherence to scientific standards. Peer review is an essential part of the scientific process and helps maintain the rigor and integrity of scientific research.

Reproducibility: The ability of an experiment or study to be repeated or replicated by other researchers, yielding consistent results. Reproducibility is a fundamental principle of science, as it ensures the reliability and validity of scientific findings.

Falsifiability: The property of a scientific hypothesis or theory that can be proven false or contradicted by empirical evidence. Falsifiability is crucial for distinguishing scientific claims from unfalsifiable or pseudoscientific ideas.

These terms provide a foundational understanding of the principles, methods, and processes involved in scientific inquiry. Science is a dynamic and evolving discipline that relies on empirical evidence, rigorous testing, and peer review to advance our understanding of the natural world.

Peer-Reviewed Journal: A scholarly publication where scientific research articles are evaluated by independent experts in the field before they are published. Peer-reviewed journals ensure the quality and credibility of scientific research.

Control Group: A group in an experiment that serves as a baseline or comparison to the experimental group. The control group is not exposed to the independent variable being tested, allowing researchers to assess the effects of the variable more accurately.

Statistical Analysis: The use of mathematical and statistical methods to analyze and interpret data in scientific research. Statistical analysis helps identify patterns, trends, and relationships within the data and provides a basis for drawing valid conclusions.

Scientific Consensus: The collective agreement among scientists in a particular field based on a substantial body of evidence. Scientific consensus represents the prevailing view or understanding supported by the majority of experts in a given area of study.

Replication: The process of conducting a study or experiment again, following the same procedures and protocols, to verify and validate previous findings. Replication is an important step in scientific inquiry to ensure the reliability and generalizability of results.

Peer-Reviewed Conference: A scientific conference where research papers are subjected to peer review before they are accepted for presentation. Peer-reviewed conferences provide opportunities for researchers to share and discuss their work with peers in their field.

Ethics in Science: The principles and guidelines that govern the responsible conduct of scientific research. Ethical considerations in science involve ensuring the well-being of human subjects, humane treatment of animals, and integrity in data collection and reporting.

Paradigm Shift: A significant change in scientific thought, theories, or approaches that revolutionize a particular field. Paradigm shifts occur when new discoveries or evidence challenge and replace existing scientific paradigms.

Scientific Literacy: The understanding of scientific concepts, processes, and methods necessary to engage with and evaluate scientific information. Scientific literacy enables individuals to critically assess scientific claims, make informed decisions, and participate in scientific discourse.

Interdisciplinary: The integration of knowledge, methods, and perspectives from multiple scientific disciplines to address complex research questions or problems. Interdisciplinary approaches encourage collaboration and the exchange of ideas across different fields of study.

These additional terms delve deeper into various aspects of scientific research, including research validation, ethics, communication, and interdisciplinary collaboration. Understanding these terms enhances one's comprehension of the scientific process, the importance of rigorous methodologies, and the broader context in which scientific knowledge is generated and shared.

Publication Bias: The selective publication of research results based on their statistical significance or perceived importance.

Publication bias can lead to an overrepresentation of positive or significant findings, while null or negative results may remain unpublished, skewing the scientific literature.

Confirmation Bias: The tendency to seek, interpret, or favor information that confirms existing beliefs or hypotheses while disregarding or downplaying contradictory evidence. Confirmation bias can lead researchers to unconsciously favor data that supports their preconceived notions, potentially introducing bias into their findings.

Sampling Bias: A bias that occurs when the sample used in a study does not accurately represent the population of interest, leading to skewed or unrepresentative results. Sampling bias can arise from non-random selection or inadequate sample size, compromising the generalizability of research findings.

Funding Bias: Bias that may result from financial interests or conflicts of interest related to funding sources. Funding bias can influence the design, execution, or reporting of research, potentially compromising objectivity and integrity.

Reporting Bias: The selective reporting or omission of data or outcomes within a study, which can lead to a distorted or incomplete representation of the research findings. Reporting bias can occur in the form of cherry-picking favorable results or suppressing unfavorable findings.

Researcher Bias: Bias introduced by researchers themselves due to personal beliefs, preferences, or vested interests. Researcher bias can affect study design, data collection, analysis, and interpretation, potentially influencing the outcome of the research.

Institutional Bias: Bias that arises from systemic practices, policies, or cultural norms within scientific institutions that favor certain methodologies, topics, or perspectives. Institutional bias can influence research priorities, publication practices, and the recognition of different research contributions.

Methodological Bias: Bias resulting from flaws or limitations in the research design, measurement tools, or data collection procedures. Methodological bias can affect the validity and reliability of research findings and may lead to inaccurate or misleading conclusions.

Socio Cultural Bias: Bias that stems from societal or cultural factors, such as prevailing ideologies, values, or power dynamics, which can shape the questions asked, methods employed, or interpretations made in scientific research. Sociocultural bias can influence research agendas and perpetuate systemic inequalities.

Peer Review Bias: Bias introduced during the peer review process, where reviewers may hold biases based on personal beliefs, disciplinary perspectives, or intellectual traditions. Peer review bias can affect the acceptance, rejection, or interpretation of research manuscripts.

Understanding bias in science is crucial for critically evaluating research findings and ensuring the integrity and reliability of scientific knowledge. These terms highlight different forms of bias that can emerge at various stages of the scientific process, shedding light on potential sources of distortion and prompting a more discerning approach to scientific inquiry.

Experimenter Bias: Bias introduced by the researchers themselves during the conduct of an experiment, where their expectations or preconceptions influence the outcome. Experimenter bias can unintentionally affect data collection, analysis, or interpretation, compromising the objectivity of the study.

Cultural Bias: Bias that arises from cultural assumptions, norms, or values that may influence the design, execution, or interpretation of scientific research. Cultural bias can lead to the underrepresentation or misrepresentation of certain groups or perspectives in scientific studies.

Gender Bias: Bias resulting from unequal treatment, stereotyping, or discrimination based on gender in scientific research. Gender bias can manifest in various ways, such as disparities in funding, publication rates, or career advancement opportunities.

Language Bias: Bias that occurs when research is predominantly published or conducted in a particular language, leading to a limited representation of diverse perspectives and findings from other language communities.

Time-Period Bias: Bias that arises from the influence of specific historical or temporal contexts on scientific research. Time-period bias can affect the questions asked, methodologies used, or interpretations made, potentially limiting the applicability or generalizability of research findings across different time periods.

Political Bias: Bias resulting from political affiliations, ideologies, or pressures that may influence the conduct, interpretation, or reporting of scientific research. Political bias can shape research agendas, funding priorities, or the dissemination of scientific information.

Industry Bias: Bias introduced when research is funded or influenced by industries with a vested interest in certain outcomes that align with their commercial objectives. Industry bias can potentially lead to conflicts of interest, selective reporting, or manipulation of research findings.

Geographical Bias: Bias that arises from a disproportionate focus on certain geographical regions or locations in scientific research. Geographical bias can result in a limited understanding of phenomena or issues specific to underrepresented regions.

File Drawer Effect: The phenomenon where studies with non-significant or inconclusive results are less likely to be published or reported, leading to an overemphasis on studies with positive or significant findings. The file drawer effect can skew the overall scientific literature, as unpublished studies can be important in understanding the full range of evidence.

Cognitive Bias: Bias that arises from inherent cognitive tendencies, such as heuristics, framing effects, or availability bias, which can influence the way scientists perceive, interpret, or remember information. Cognitive biases can unintentionally affect scientific reasoning and decision-making.

Population: The entire group of individuals, objects, or events that a researcher is interested in studying. The population represents the complete set of elements to which statistical inferences are made.

Sample: A subset of the population selected for study. Samples are used to gather data and make inferences about the larger population. The sample should be representative of the population to ensure the generalizability of the findings.

Variable: A characteristic or attribute that can vary or take on different values. Variables can be quantitative (numeric) or qualitative (categorical) and are the building blocks for statistical analysis.

Descriptive Statistics: Statistical methods used to summarize and describe the main features of data. Descriptive statistics provide measures such as mean, median, mode, standard deviation, and graphical representations to present data in a meaningful and concise manner.

Inferential Statistics: Statistical methods used to draw conclusions or make predictions about a population based on sample data. Inferential statistics involve hypothesis testing, estimation, and generalization from the sample to the population.

Probability: A measure of the likelihood of an event occurring. Probability is expressed as a number between 0 and 1, where 0 represents impossibility, and 1 represents certainty. Probability forms the foundation of statistical inference and helps quantify uncertainty.

Hypothesis Testing: A statistical procedure used to evaluate the plausibility of a claim or hypothesis about a population based on sample data. Hypothesis testing involves formulating null and alternative hypotheses, conducting a statistical test, and interpreting the results.

Confidence Interval: A range of values computed from sample data that is likely to contain the true value of a population parameter with a certain level of confidence. Confidence intervals provide a measure of the precision or uncertainty associated with parameter estimation.

Regression Analysis: A statistical technique used to explore the relationship between a dependent variable and one or more independent variables. Regression analysis helps identify and quantify the strength and direction of the relationship between variables.

Statistical Significance: The likelihood that an observed result is not due to random chance but is a real effect. Statistical significance is usually assessed by comparing the observed data to a null hypothesis and determining the probability of obtaining such extreme results if the null hypothesis were true.

These terms provide a foundational understanding of statistical concepts and methods. Statistics play a crucial role in data analysis, research interpretation, decision-making, and drawing meaningful conclusions from data.

Sampling Bias: Bias that occurs when the sample used in a study is not representative of the population of interest. Sampling bias can result in skewed or unrepresentative data and lead to inaccurate or misleading conclusions.

Nonresponse Bias: Bias that arises when individuals selected for a study do not respond or participate, leading to a biased sample. Nonresponse bias can affect the validity and generalizability of the study's findings.

Measurement Bias: Bias that occurs when the measurement instrument or procedure consistently produces results that differ from the true value. Measurement bias can introduce systematic errors and distort the interpretation of data.

Reporting Bias: Bias resulting from the selective reporting or omission of data or outcomes in statistical analysis or research. Reporting bias can lead to an inaccurate representation of the findings, favoring certain results over others.

Observer Bias: Bias introduced by the subjective judgments, expectations, or interpretations of the observer or researcher. Observer bias can influence the recording, classification, or interpretation of data, potentially leading to biased conclusions.

Confounding Bias: Bias that arises when an extraneous variable or factor is associated with both the independent and dependent variables, leading to a spurious or misleading relationship. Confounding bias can distort the true cause-and-effect relationship being investigated.

Publication Bias: Bias resulting from the selective publication of research findings based on their statistical significance or perceived importance. Publication bias can lead to an overrepresentation of positive or significant results, while null or negative findings may remain unpublished, skewing the overall evidence.

Volunteer Bias: Bias that occurs when individuals who volunteer to participate in a study differ systematically from the general population, leading to an unrepresentative sample. Volunteer bias can impact the external validity and generalizability of the findings.

Recall Bias: Bias that arises from errors or distortions in

Fun and Easy Way to Detect Bias (spin) in the News:

The first step to understanding how to detect bias in the news is to understand that it exists, and that most news agencies have a political agenda they are trying to promote in some way, whether liberal, conservative, progressive, reactionary, etc.

The first step to understanding political bias in the news is to be able to identify the power players, and their backers and what is their motivation. What do they want?

Let us imagine the news is reporting a story about a community who doesn't want a prison built in their town. So, the power players are probably the people of the community vs. the forces who want a prison built. This could be the prison building company, the government, people from other communities who don't care, etc.

Once you have identified the power players and what their motivation is, then it is simply a matter of figuring out which team the author of the article or the news agency is rooting for? Frequently this will be apparent in the way the article is framed starting with the headline.

Consider, for example, the following:

The Community Doesn't Want a Prison Built Near Where their Children Go to School.

Vs.

Local Residents Resistant to Correctional Facility Despite Overwhelming State Support.

Each of these is talking about the same issue, but already by the frame we can tell bias toward one side or the other. In the first example I used the word Prison because it has a negative connotation with crime: I also chose to add the emotionally charged word "Children," so that my reader would want to protect the children from crime.

In the second example, I didn't use the word "Prison" and instead used "Correctional Facility," which sounds more gentle, and has a more positive connotation. I also used the phrase "Overwhelming State Support," to imply Local residents seem like they are the bad guys going against the will of the majority.

A more dialectic or less bias frame in the headline would be something like:

Community Members and State Officials Weigh in on Prison Issue

This would require me to have to read the article in order to detect bias. The thing I am now looking for is any favoritism toward one side or the other: which side gets more of their point of view shared?
And, most importantly, look at how the article ends. The ending is the last word, so if you can see how it favors one side or the other, it may be biased toward that side.

How do deal with more complex issues, such as, Immigration, Syria, the Israel Palestine Conflict:

You deal with it in the same way, however, there will be more variables, more power players.

But here is how you basically sort out the teams:

Who is in power? What do they want? (Explicitly and Implicitly) Who is challenging their power? What do they want? (Explicitly and Implicitly?) Who are the other factions involved and who are they loyal to?

Then, of course, which side is the news organization on? Who are they loyal to?

Homework: write out your answers in complete sentences!

Go to any mainstream corporate news source: Fox, CNN, MSNBC, etc. Find an article on a domestic issue that is political and by political I mean there is a power struggle involved, and not just something about Justin Beiber's hair.

Identify the power players.

Identify a framing bias if there is one in the title.

Identify which side you think the newspaper article is on and why. What are the implications of the article or what we would ideally do as a result of it? Give a quote of support.

Notes on how to read science:

Trying to figure out whether or not I should take fish oils. After trying to look more seriously into the "truth" about fish oil supplementation, I have run into many of the problems of our current post-truth era. First of all, when I went looking for primary source material i.e. studies about fish oil, I had to first focus my search on one area. I chose to look at its effect on cognitive ability. The first study I looked at was so complex I would need some statistical knowledge in order to read it accurately.

Here is a sample:

A multicenter placebo-controlled double-blind randomized trial was conducted between 2012 and 2013. Cognitive function was assessed at baseline and after one year using 4 neuropsychological tests. Nutritional status was assessed using Mini Nutritional Assessment (MNA). Interaction between Mini-Mental State Examination (MMSE) score and nutritional status were analyzed using linear regression models.

Since I don't know was being tested in the neuropsychological tests, nor what a linear regression model is, I skipped to the conclusion which stated:

Supplementation with n-3 PUFA did not show an improvement in the global cognitive function in institutionalized elderly people without CI or with MCI. They only suggest an apparent improvement in memory loss if previously they were well nourished.

The last sentence is so confusing unto itself I began to feel sad.

I went to some other secondary websites to see if they could sum things up for me better, but I was also wary of the commercial influence that some of these websites might have, such as being funded by the Big Fish Oil, which I am sure is a very lucrative business with a lot at stake in terms of wanting to prove its efficacy, and brand as a kind of cure all.

I should note here that just as in other forms of propaganda we can divide this issue into two camps in order to understand the bias. On the one hand we would have the idea that fish oil can cure everything and, on the other hand, we would have the idea that fish oil is completely useless.

Here is where a little common sense comes in handy. My common sense tells me that since fish is a natural food (at least in theory) that has been eaten for probably as long as humans have been eating, that it is probably not bad for you when eaten in moderation. In addition, since I don't eat any fish because I don't like the taste, then it makes sense to me that adding some fish oil to my diet might be a good thing. As with all vitamin issues, however, there comes the question of whether taking it in a supplemental pill form is as effective as taking it in a natural form.

Here is what I found on that subject:

Omega-3 food sources vs. supplements

Can omega-3 benefits preserve thinking skills? The evidence is encouraging, at least when the omega-3s come from food. A notable five-year observational study, published online in Neurology May 4, 2016, found that older adults who ate at least one seafood meal per week performed better on thinking skills tests during the study period than people who ate less than one seafood meal per week. People who carried the APOE4 gene variant (which increases Alzheimer's disease risk) appeared to benefit even more from diets rich in omega-3 fats. It doesn't prove that eating fish helped maintain thinking skills, but the evidence is reasonably strong that it may.

The evidence is not as encouraging about the value of omega-3s in pills, such as fish oil supplements. One of the largest and longest randomized trials, published Aug. 25, 2015, in The Journal of the American Medical Association (JAMA), was part of a larger study to find out if nutrients help delay vision loss. Researchers followed 4,000 older adults over five years. Some took fish oil pills, and some didn't. All participants had tests of their thinking skills during the study, and test scores in both groups decreased similarly over time, suggesting the fish oil didn't slow any decline in thinking skills. Similarly, a study of DHA in people with mild to moderate Alzheimer's dementia, published in JAMA Nov. 3, 2010, demonstrated no benefits.

Though this is a summary of the findings, at least it cited the primary sources, which I could look up if I had more time and inclination. This leads me to my next point, which is the sheer amount of work it takes to look up a credible source on something as simple as fish oil.

It made me realize how much we depend on secondary sources and experts for our opinion, and consequently how vulnerable many people are to oversimplified advertisements masquerading as hard science.

As I was trying to get answers, I also ran into another issue, which relates back to the concept of how to frame an issue. I began by framing my issue as: "What is the effect of fish oil on cognitive ability?" And though evidence of this was difficult, there seemed to be more evidence to support that it does help reduce inflammation, which has been shown to help with cognitive ability. This is when I realized I was done for the day, but I want to point out some things to consider.

First of all, I would like to start with the good news. As an undergraduate, students are not expected to understand all the nuances of a scientific study, and if I were writing an undergraduate paper on "the effects of fish oil on cognitive ability," it would be very easy to find simple points of data either for or against the argument. I could simply cherry pick the studies that conform to my confirmation bias or needs of my thesis.

The bad news is that as somebody trying to figure out whether or not I should take fish oil to improve my health, it takes a lot of work, and in the end, my decision will be made by less scientific and more personal means. As I mentioned in the previous paper, the last time I took fish oils, I felt dizzy, and so I am not excited to try them again, but I am not 100% sure they were the cause of my dizziness. Despite the conflicting evidence about the efficacy of fish oil in regard to cognitive function, I have found enough evidence to suggest its usefulness in some capacity for me to want to take it as long as it doesn't make me dizzy or taste fish. Consequently, I can now research alternative forms of it, and proceed from there, but I am not looking forward to it.

In conclusion, here is an example of a scientific study done at the University of Pittsburgh that isn't quite as complex to read as the one I showed earlier, though it may have similar issues. Here are the general things I look for.

Who is the "control group" or people taking part in the study? What might be the hidden variables? Was there a placebo group?

Here is a copy of the study:

Omega-3 fatty acids (fish oil) as an anti-inflammatory: an alternative to nonsteroidal anti-inflammatory drugs for discogenic pain.

Maroon JC1, Bost JW.
Author information
1
Department of Neurological Surgery, University of Pittsburgh Medical Center, Pittsburgh, PA, USA. maroonjc@upmc.edu
Abstract
BACKGROUND:

The use of NSAID medications is a well-established effective therapy for both acute and chronic nonspecific neck and back pain. Extreme complications, including gastric ulcers, bleeding, myocardial infarction, and even deaths, are associated with their use. An alternative treatment with fewer side effects that also reduces the inflammatory response and thereby reduces pain is believed to be omega-3 EFAs found in fish oil. We report our experience in a neurosurgical practice using fish oil supplements for pain relief.

METHODS:
From March to June 2004, 250 patients who had been seen by a neurosurgeon and were found to have nonsurgical neck or back pain were asked to take a total of 1200 mg per day of omega-3 EFAs (eicosapentaenoic acid and docosahexaenoic acid) found in fish oil supplements. A questionnaire was sent approximately 1 month after starting the supplement.

RESULTS:

Of the 250 patients, 125 returned the questionnaire at an average of 75 days on fish oil. Seventy-eight percent were taking 1200 mg and 22% were taking 2400 mg of EFAs. Fifty-nine percent discontinued to take their prescription NSAID medications for pain. Sixty percent stated that their overall pain had improved, and 60% stated that their joint pain had improved. Eighty percent stated they were satisfied with their improvement, and 88% stated they would continue to take the fish oil. There were no significant side effects reported.

CONCLUSIONS:

Our results mirror other controlled studies that compared ibuprofen and omega-3 EFAs demonstrating equivalent effect in reducing arthritic pain. omega-3 EFA fish oil supplements appear to be a safer alternative to NSAIDs for treatment of nonsurgical neck or back pain in this selective group.

The Importance of Using Credible Sources in College Papers

Academic writing is a rigorous endeavor that demands precision, clarity, and above all, credibility. The foundation of any solid research paper lies not just in the originality of the idea or argument, but in the quality of sources used to support that argument. Utilizing credible sources lends authority, depth, and trustworthiness to a student's work. Here is a detailed exploration of why credible sources are indispensable in college papers and where students can find them.

1. Maintaining Academic Integrity:

Using credible sources is essential for maintaining academic integrity. Plagiarism, the act of presenting someone else's ideas or words as one's own, is a grave academic offense. Utilizing reliable and properly cited sources ensures that credit is given where it's due. This not only prevents accusations of plagiarism but also positions the student as an honest and responsible researcher.

2. Establishing Authority and Trustworthiness:
An argument is only as strong as the evidence supporting it. Drawing from established and credible sources ensures that the evidence is both trustworthy and relevant. An essay citing well-respected experts in the field will always have a stronger impact than one relying on dubious or unknown sources.

3. Ensuring Accuracy of Information:
In the age of the internet, information is abundant, but not all of it is accurate. Using credible sources ensures that the information presented in the paper is factually accurate, thereby preventing the spread of misinformation.

4. Enhancing Critical Thinking Skills:
The process of evaluating and selecting credible sources hones a student's critical thinking skills. It challenges them to discern the reliability and relevance of information, pushing them to become better, more discerning researchers.

Where to Find Credible Sources:

Academic Libraries: These are treasure troves of credible information. Most college campuses have their own libraries stocked with books, journals, and other academic materials relevant to various courses.

Online Scholarly Databases: Websites like Google Scholar, JSTOR, and PubMed offer a vast array of peer-reviewed articles, journals, and papers from various disciplines.

Academic Journals: These are periodicals dedicated to specific fields of study, and the articles within them are typically peer-reviewed, ensuring their credibility. Examples include the 'Journal of Clinical Psychology' or 'Nature'.

Government Websites: Websites ending in '.gov' often provide statistics, studies, and official information. For example, the World Health Organization (WHO) or the Centers for Disease Control and Prevention (CDC) are reliable sources for health-related topics.

University Websites: Websites ending in '.edu' can also provide valuable information, especially when they host academic publications or research conducted by faculty and students.

Renowned Research Institutions: Organizations like the Pew Research Center or the Rand Corporation often conduct studies on various topics and can be an excellent source of credible information.

In conclusion, the importance of using credible sources in college papers cannot be overstated. It ensures the accuracy, integrity, and strength of a student's work, and in the process, elevates the quality of discourse in academia. As researchers, students have a responsibility to present information that is not only compelling but also trustworthy, and relying on credible sources is the surest way to achieve this standard.

Engaging in effective research requires familiarity with a range of terms that pertain to the methods, approaches, and processes involved. Here's a list of key terms that are crucial for understanding the nuances of research:

Abstract: A brief summary of a research article, thesis, or review, which provides an overview of the main points, purpose, and conclusions.

Bibliography: A list of the books, articles, and other sources used in a research work.

Citation: A reference to a source of information, typically formatted according to a specific style guide (e.g., APA, MLA, Chicago).

Variable: Any factor, trait, or condition that can exist in differing amounts or types. This includes dependent, independent, and controlled variables.

Hypothesis: A tentative, testable statement or prediction about what one expects to observe in research.

Methodology: The system of methods and principles used in a particular discipline.

Qualitative Research: Research that deals with descriptions and data that can be observed but not measured, such as interviews or observations.

Quantitative Research: Research that deals with numbers and statistical data.

Sample: A subset of a population chosen for a study to represent the whole population.

Population: The entire group that a researcher is interested in, from which a sample might be drawn.

Control Group: In experimental research, the group that does not receive the treatment and is used as a benchmark to measure the effects of the treatment.

Experimental Group: In experimental research, the group that receives the treatment or intervention.

Peer Review: A process by which research is evaluated by experts in the same field before being published.

Primary Source: An original source that has not been previously published or interpreted, like original research, diaries, interviews, and historical documents.

Secondary Source: Describes or analyzes primary sources, including books or articles that interpret, review, or synthesize original research/primary sources.

Validity: The extent to which a tool, test, or research study measures what it intends to measure.

Reliability: The consistency and stability of a measure over time.

Bias: Any systematic error that affects the results of a study, making them not generalizable to the wider population.

Ethics: The standards of behavior and conduct in research, ensuring that researchers act in ways that are professional, fair, and respectful to all involved.

Understanding these terms can greatly aid in comprehending, conducting, and evaluating research across a wide range of fields.

Determining the credibility of a source is essential for producing accurate, reliable, and high-quality research or content. Understanding the following key terms can help in evaluating the trustworthiness of sources:

Primary Source: Direct or firsthand evidence about an event, object, person, or work of art, including historical and legal documents, eyewitness accounts, and experimental data.

Secondary Source: Materials that interpret, critique, or analyze primary sources, such as books or articles that review original research.

Tertiary Source: Reference materials that consolidate primary and secondary sources into a summarized form, like encyclopedias or textbooks.

Peer Review: A process by which manuscripts, studies, or articles are assessed by experts in the same field before publication, ensuring quality and credibility.

Bias: A particular preference or point of view that may skew information. Recognizing potential biases can help in assessing the objectivity of a source.

Citation: A reference to a published or unpublished source, providing the necessary details to locate the original material.

Scholarly/Academic Article: A publication written by and for experts in a particular discipline, often peer-reviewed.

Editorial Review: A review process where editors or advisory boards review content before publication. While not as rigorous as peer review, it still offers a degree of validation.

Abstract: A brief summary at the beginning of academic articles, which provides an overview of the study or research.

Bibliography/References: Lists of sources or citations at the end of a book or article, which can be useful in gauging the depth and quality of the research.

Corroboration: Confirmation or support from other sources. Credible information often can be corroborated by multiple reputable sources.

Publication Date: The date when the content was published. It's essential to ensure that information, especially in rapidly changing fields, is current.

Author Affiliation: The institution or organization with which the author is associated, which can lend credibility based on the reputation of the institution.

Impact Factor: A measure of how often an academic journal article is cited, indicating its influence or importance in the field.

Credentials: The qualifications or background of an author or creator, which can provide context about their expertise.

Retraction: The removal of a published study, typically due to errors or ethical concerns, which is a mark against the source's credibility.

Open Source: Materials that are freely accessible and might not undergo traditional peer review, making verification essential.

Domain: The suffix of a website's URL (e.g., .edu, .gov, .com) can give hints about the nature of the site and its potential credibility.

Reproducibility: The ability of an experiment or study to be reproduced by other researchers, reinforcing its credibility.

Anecdotal Evidence: Personal stories or examples. While they can be genuine and compelling, they are not a replacement for comprehensive, evidence-based research.

Understanding these terms will empower you to critically assess and determine the credibility of sources across various platforms and disciplines.

Key to my comments on papers:

When I read a paper, I am looking primarily for your ability to articulate yourself at the level of writing where you are at, and consequently, my attention to grammar and detail will be in service of this ideal. In other words, my job is to make your paper as smooth as possible, according to your ability level, voice, and natural writing style, while at the same time pushing you toward more complex forms of written expression.

Indent five spaces for paragraph

Put this here

Keep in either present tense or past tense. This means you are shifting tenses as you write and it sounds like this: "I went to the movies with my brother and we get some popcorn…" Choose one, and stick to it; make it consistent. "I went to the movies with my brother and we got some popcorn…"

A paragraph is needed because there is a shift in either TIME or SUBJECT MATTER

This means that something is improperly spelled or punctuated, and that it is up to you to figure out what the problem is and correct it.

Awkward sentence: This means that if I work really hard I can kind of understand what you are trying to say, but it is sloppily written, sometimes too long and wordy; other times you yourself haven't figured out what you are saying yet.

The basic remedy: Imagine I asked you to tell me out loud what you are trying to say here; then write down whatever words you would use to explain it to me in person. This usually does the trick or gets you much closer to what you're trying to say.

What does this mean? : This means that the writing is so sloppy I have no clue of what you are trying to say, and I have a hunch that you do not either, so employ the aforementioned method, and tell me again what it is you are trying to say here. Imagine you are telling me in person and transcribing your words; a lot of times things get lost in translation from verbal to written, so it helps to think of it as verbal and just transcribe it to written.

Transition: This means you need a sentence that tells me where we have been and where we are going, so that I can relax; if you have taken me from one topic to the next without a transition of some kind, it can feel like you are taking me on a wild goose chase, even if it all comes together in the end. In academic writing especially, it is important to let your reader know you have everything under control.

Reiterate Relevance or remind me of what your overall point is: Tell me again how this relates to the overall point you are trying to make, so that the reader sees the relevance of the information you just gave. This helps keep focus for the reader and the writers, so that you know what to include and what not to include.

If it doesn't relate to the overall point, cut it.

CUT: This means to cut something because it is either irrelevant, redundant, or doesn't add anything significant to the point you are trying to make.

Sometimes I will have you cut and paste something, and this will be indicated by a bracket [passage], and the letter, A, B, or C following it. I will then indicate that the bracketed passage A should be cut and pasted somewhere else in the essay, indicated by the phrase: PUT A HERE.

More here: This means you have started to say something interesting, but you cut yourself off before truly exploring what you are trying to say, so please add more about what you are saying here so that I can get a more full explanation of your idea or concept.

Word Choice: This means that you have a word here that isn't quite the right word for the job or it is off key from the rest of the writing and needs to be traded for a word that is more tonally appropriate.

Terms dealing especially with personal essay:

Intro: This person, place, or thing needs an introduction, telling the reader what the deal with it is, the history of your relationship, how you feel about this, etc. This gives the reader, who does not know your life story, context, so that they can go into the story knowing a bit about why the story you're going to tell is important. See the first chapter on how to write personal narratives for more explanation.

Context simply means giving background info so that the reader is on board with you.
Specific Example: You are generalizing, and need to give a specific example to illustrate what you are talking about: See the many handouts I gave on this if you need more specifics on what a specific example looks like.

Inner Response: You are talking about specific incidents, but you are not telling me how you are feeling about this incident, what is going on in your head at the time it is happening. This shows me what is at stake for you, why it is important. See the many handouts I have given to see how important this is to personal writing.

Dialogue: dialogue would be very useful here because of what is being said, and how important it is to the story.

=you made a good point here, interesting, insightful, funny, or you gave a strong example or evidence to support a point.

= you said something here that was shocking or attention grabbing.

Keep in mind that when you revise a paper, it's not just about doing the bare minimum of what I've corrected, but really going back in and re-reading your paper, and asking yourself how can I make this better in light of the feedback I received. A bare minimum approach to revision, seldom yields a higher grade.

I grade papers on the following 3 criteria: In order to receive an A you would have to be high in at least two of these categories.

Fluency: this is how well the paper is put together, and flows without errors in grammar and punctuation. This is about how easy it is for me to read without having to stop to figure out what is being said.

Structure and reasoning: this is how well your paper is organized and articulated with a clear purpose, and supported with credible sources. This is making sure the reader knows what it is you're trying to accomplish in your paper, and knowing at all times where we are in that process.

Courage, originality and insight: this means writing something with a new angle or talking about something that requires courage and/or vulnerability. This means coming up with new ideas or new ways of looking at something. This means writing with extra grace, humor, or style.

If you received an in-between grade such as A/A- that means I couldn't determine one or the other, and I will change it depending on whether you revise the paper or what you get on the next graded assignment. Let's imagine you don't revise this paper, then get an A on your next paper, then I would round up and give you an A for both. Or conversely, if you got another A- then I would give you an A- for both.

Run on sentences and comma splices:

How do you know when to use a comma or a period or a semicolon?

Let's start with looking at the question of whether or not to use a comma or a period.

Generally speaking you put a period after a complete sentence.

What is a complete sentence?

When there is a subject and a verb or in other words when somebody does something.

Here are some complete sentences:

He ate.

He ate the apple.

Things get a little more tricky as the sentence gets longer.

He ate the apple, it was delicious.

Now, for some reason, we are not supposed to break up two complete sentences with a comma. This is called a comma splice, but you can if you put an and in there:

He ate the apple, and it was delicious.

Don't ask me why, as both sound okay to me.

If we think of a comma as being a short pause, and a period as being a longer pause,
however, I can see how it might become an issue with longer sentences, such as this one:

He ate the apple, and it was delicious, the taste reminded him of grandmother's pie, he smiled.

This, to me, sounds garbled with so many commas, and I would want to break it up with a longer pause so it would sound better.

He ate the apple, and it was delicious. The taste reminded him of his grandmother's pie. He smiled.

I could also write:

He ate the apple. It was delicious. The taste reminded him of grandma's pie. He smiled.

This one, however, sounds too choppy for my taste, even though it isn't grammatically incorrect.

Rewrite the following sentences to sound right to your ear:

I went to the baseball game, found my brother Henry asleep beneath the bleachers, I shook him, he opened his eyes, the night was just beginning.

Doctors have discovered a cure for onion tears, it's a new pill that blocks tear ducts, it has worked on rats in the lab, there is a 100% success rate.

My mom is so kind, she gives me cookies and milk, she mows the lawn for me, she gives me one hundred dollar bills when I say the word, "Hundo"

High school was rough, constant punches, weed, teachers.

Statistics show that 9 out of ten mothers choose Skippy Brand Peanut Butter over Jif, after being blindfolded and given spoons, the mothers liked the Skippy, they said it tasted like a dream.

Here is a run on sentence. Fix it.

We went to camping the other day with my brother Mike, and it was warm and sunny, and we ate a bunch of potato chips, and Mike got sick when he had a bad chip that was green, and he should have known better because no potato chip is green, but he started vomiting all right, right in the tent, and that is when I got to feeling kind of sick myself.

Random handouts, key terms, and assignments that are still being sorted:

Miscellaneous terms, handouts, and assignments:

Find your aesthetic part #1:

aes·thet·ic
/esˈTHedik/

adjective
concerned with beauty or the appreciation of beauty.
"the pictures give great aesthetic pleasure"
noun
a set of principles underlying and guiding the work of a particular artist or artistic movement.

"the Cubist aesthetic"

Although the primary focus in this class will be on poetry, I think it is also important to see how poetry can relate to other genres of art, and the world at large. One of the things I was able to do when I was in graduate school was look at what might be called my "aesthetic," that is to say, what my artistic taste is. I had never really thought about it before, but I came to understand very quickly how important it is for any artist to know what their aesthetic is. Even though you may not be able to articulate what your aesthetic/s is right now, and it may evolve over time, I think it's important to start figuring it out now so that you can better guide your work and aspirations. Eventually, I am going to ask you to articulate two aesthetics you might have, so that you might be able to combine them, but for now I want you to be able to articulate just one to the best of your ability.

First I am going to talk a little about my aesthetic, and how I came to know what it is. As I said earlier, prior to my going to graduate school in poetry, I had no idea what having an "aesthetic" meant, and when I was asked I said something like, I don't know. I guess I like things that are funny and absurd.

That was all I knew. Over time, however, I came to realize that many funny and absurd works of art come out of art movements such as DADA, and Surrealism, and the further I looked in that direction, the more I saw other artists who shared my sensibilities. This wasn't the only kind of poetry I liked, of course, as I appreciated all different kinds of poetry, but this was definitely a direction I wanted to explore.

So how can you start figuring out your aesthetic?

First, make a list of your ten favorite works of art. This doesn't have to be fiction, but can also be poetry, films, songs, paintings, etc.

Now, ask yourself what is it you like about each one, it could be it makes you laugh, it makes you think of something personal, etc.

Identify any qualities that these works might have in common such as theme, tone, style, subject matter.

Ask yourself what life experiences might have led you to this aesthetic?

Here would have been my list at the time I was asked:

Kafka's Metamorphosis: made me use my imagination, and see something unreal.

Monty Python and the Holy Grail among others: made me laugh at the absurdity of life.

Salvador Dali's melting clocks: made me use my imagination, and see the world differently.

George Carlin's stand up comedy: made me laugh at the hypocrisy of life

Andy Kaufman's stand up comedy: made me laugh at the conventions of performance.

Tim and Eric Awesome Show Great Job (If it had existed at the time) made me laugh at the absurdity of modern life.

What are some of the collective values of the aesthetic? What does it care about and why?

For me, the values were dream-like images, absurd humor, and unexpected twists as well as nonsense, brevity, and wit, and fabulist stories that exposed some hypocrisy in society.

In terms of life experiences, I suppose growing up with an alcoholic father who had a wonderfully absurd sense of humor influenced my taste quite a bit. In addition, my mother's side of the family also valued humor as a way to deal with life's difficulties.

Once, I had established some artists, works, and values of my aesthetic, then I would look to see what or who were their influences? This might take a little research, reading interviews, etc. but it is fascinating to see how artists learn and grow from other artists.

This is how I discovered other writers, poets, and artists who had influenced each other and been parts of movements such as DADA, surrealism, and Magic Realism.
Part two will be two identifying genius examples, and finding another aesthetic since we seldom like just one kind of art.

Ultimately, we will want to find poets, but when we are just beginning, I think it is important to look at a variety of genres because you, like me, may not have had the time to figure that out.

Once, I had established some artists, works, and values of my aesthetic, then I would look to see what or who were their influences? This might take a little research, reading interviews, etc. but it is fascinating to see how artists learn and grow from other artists.

This is how I discovered other writers, poets, and artists who had influenced each other and been parts of movements such as DADA, surrealism, and Magic Realism.

The last step will be finding specifically the poets who share this aesthetic, as well as being able to identify the most inspirational and genius examples of it.

Be your own Chat Gpt: How to translate common mundane tasks into sexy attention grabbing phrases.

Honestly, Open AI is fantastic for writing formal letters, but you still need to tailor them to your own needs, and know what the words mean in case you have to articulate yourself in an interview.

Keywords for resumes and cover letters for power translations:

I washed dishes and stacked them back on the rack.

Utilized machinery to facilitate the cleanliness of all vital utensils.

Oversaw the optimization of operational hygiene according to protocol.

I listened to the wait staff tell me when they needed a table cleared.

Communicated with staff to ensure proper logistical support in daily operations.

I told the manager when we were out of soap.

Corresponded regularly with management to ensure supply chain efficacy.

I stacked boxes of shoes and made sure that they were in the right place.

Organized and facilitated proper inventory protocol to maximize sales efficiency.

I wrote down inventory and made sure the manager knew when we were running low on a certain shoe.

Anticipated inventory shortfalls and communicated with management to ensure optimal efficiency.

I helped customers find a shoe that fits them.

Collaborated closely with customers to ensure ideal customer satisfaction.

I rang up customers at the cash register.

Facilitated purchases with computational competency.

I answer questions about shoes over the phone to get sales.

Educated customers about products to ensure maximum productivity.

I wrote a paper comparing two philosophers views of education

Authored a comparative analysis of contrasting educational ideologies.

I summarized a bunch of different essays.

Synthesized key points in a variety of modalities.

I used a bunch of new vocabulary words to show I understood how they were used.

Demonstrated facility with nomenclature appropriate to a wide variety of disciplines.

I wrote personal essays reflecting on how my life related to certain topics.

Integrated theoretical knowledge into a variety of practical applications.

I learned about how bottom-line thinking can be detrimental to society.

Analyzed the challenges facing capitalist ideology in contemporary society.

The following are taken from the University of Colorado Boulder Website: https://www.colorado.edu/career/job-searching/resumes-and-cover-letters/resumes/action-verbs-use-your-resume

When you created or wrote something…

Acted, Adapted, Combined, Composed, Conceptualized, Condensed, Created, Customized, Designed, Developed, Devised, Directed, Displayed, Entertained, Established, Fashioned, Formulated, Founded, Illustrated, Initiated, Instituted, Integrated, Introduced, Invented, Modeled, Modified, Originated, Performed, Photographed, Planned, Revised, Revitalized, Shaped, Solve.

When you were a research machine…

Analyzed, Clarified, Collected, Compared, Conducted, Critiqued, Detected, Determined, Diagnosed, Evaluated, Examined, Experimented, Explored, Extracted, Formulated, Gathered, Identified, Inspected, Interpreted, Interviewed, Invented, Investigated, Located, Measured, Organized, Researched, Reviewed, Searched, Solved, Summarized, Surveyed, Systematized.

When you manage a project or group...

Accomplished, Administered, Advanced, Analyzed, Appointed, Approved, Assigned, Attained, Authorized, Chaired, Considered, Consolidated, Contracted, Controlled, Converted, Coordinated, Decided, Delegated, Developed, Directed, Eliminated, Emphasized, Enforced, Enhanced, Established, Executed, Generated, Handled, Headed, Hired, Hosted, Improved, Incorporated, Increased, Initiated, Inspected, Instituted, Led, Managed, Merged, Motivated, Navigated, Organized, Originated, Overhauled, Oversaw, Planned, Presided, Prioritized, Produced, Recommended, Reorganized, Replaced, Restored, Reviewed, Scheduled, Secured, Selected, Streamlined, Strengthened, Supervised, Terminated.

When numbers and figures are your thing...

Administered, Adjusted, Allocated, Analyzed, Appraised, Assessed, Audited, Balanced, Budgeted, Calculated, Computed, Conserved, Controlled, Corrected, Decreased, Determined, Developed, Estimated, Forecasted, Managed, Marketed, Measured, Netted, Planned, Prepared, Programmed, Projected, Qualified, Reconciled, Reduced, Researched, Retrieved.

When you creatively brought an idea to life...

Acted, Adapted, Combined, Composed, Conceptualized, Condensed, Created, Customized, Designed, Developed, Devised, Directed, Displayed, Entertained, Established, Fashioned, Formulated, Founded, Illustrated, Initiated, Invented, Modeled, Modified, Originated, Performed, Photographed, Planned, Revised, Revitalized, Shaped, Solved.

When you helped with a project...

Adapted, Advocated, Aided, Answered, Arranged, Assessed, Assisted, Clarified, Coached, Collaborated, Contributed, Cooperated, Counseled, Demonstrated, Diagnosed, Educated, Encouraged, Ensured, Expedited, Facilitated, Familiarized, Furthered, Guided, Helped, Insured, Intervened, Motivated, Prevented, Provided, Referred, Rehabilitated, Represented, Resolved, Simplified, Supplied, Supported, Volunteered.

When you need to explain technical expertise...

Adapted, Applied, Assembled, Built, Calculated, Computed, Conserved, Constructed, Converted, Debugged, Designed, Determined, Developed, Engineered, Fabricated, Fortified, Installed, Maintained, Operated, Overhauled, Printed, Programmed, Rectified, Regulated, Remodeled, Repaired, Replaced, Restored, Solved, Specialized, Standardized, Studied, Upgraded, Utilized.

When you were the teacher...

Adapted, Advised, Clarified, Coached, Communicated, Conducted, Coordinated, Critiqued, Developed, Enabled, Encouraged, Evaluated, Explained, Facilitated, Focused, Guided, Individualized, Informed, Installed, Instructed, Motivated, Persuaded, Simulated, Stimulated, Taught, Tested, Trained, Transmitted, Tutored.

Jose's extras:

Followed protocols = followed procedures

Logistics = planning i.e. oversaw the logistics of the salad bar

Modalities = ways of doing things i.e. I prepared food in multiple modalities

Optimized = made optimal i.e. Optimized efficiency of the sandwich protocol.

Nomenclature = specialized language for a given field or discipline

Systemic = related to a system i.e. oversaw systemic efficiency of restaurant protocol.

Utilized = used i.e. utilized digging apparatus to excavate soil for optimal drainage

Assignment:

On a separate sheet of paper, write down ten sentences of what you do at your current or past job or both, and translate them into power sentences using as demonstrated above.

How to write a summary and symbolic analysis for narratives:

Please write double-spaced, even though I didn't:

Part 1: Plot summary

In the short story.......(Title in Capital Letters)....by... (Author)...they/he/she tells the story of (main character) and... (what is their primary struggle on a literal level?)..In the end,........how is the struggle resolved or not?...

In the short story, "Los Gamines" by Eduardo Galeano, he tells the story of a street kid named Arturo Duenas who finds a dog by accident. They become companions for a while, before Arturo gets arrested for stealing, and loses the dog, who he is unable to find him again.

Part 2: Symbolic analysis: (Use the plug-and-play method before writing. I went through two concepts (hope and friendship) before I found the one that worked best for me.)

Though there may be more than one symbol in the story, I am going to analyze the.....(concrete thing) as a symbol of....(abstract concept)

In the story, for example, when......(give an example in the story where the symbol can be read on two levels, the literal and symbolic)......................., this can read on a literal level as being about............................,but on a symbolic level it can also be read as...............................Finally, at the end of the story when.....................(talk about the last thing that happens to the symbol or when it was last mentioned) it means..................on a literal level, but metaphorically it could also mean.............................. In addition,....(explain a little more here).

Though there may be more than one symbol in the story, I am going to analyze the dog in the story as a symbol of his identity. For example, when it says, "…they look at each other, both equal, the son's of no one," it's talking literally about him and the dog, but on a metaphorical level, it could also be Arturo seeing his own identity. Consequently, at the end of the story when he loses the dog, and the writer says, "There is no one in the world quite as alone, as this boy of seven, his voice hoarse from so much yelling…" He is talking on a literal level about how lonely the boy is without his dog, but on a metaphorical level, this could also be about how lonely it is to exit without an identity. In addition, this is exactly how society sees homeless kids. They are all but invisible and don't have an identity of their own. They are orphans of a system that doesn't care about them.

Part 3: The title analysis

(Does the title add anything to the story? If so, what? If you have already analyzed the thing in the title, you can skip this, but since the title of the story is gamine, which translates to street urchin, I will say something about it.)

In looking at the title of this story................................ one can also see, one can also see a deeper meaning in how..

In looking at the title of this story "Gamine," one can also see a deeper meaning in how it relates to the theme of identity. When I translated this story from Spanish, I left the title the same because

I felt like gamine has its own meaning in Latin America, and the best translation I could find in English was "street urchin," which you don't hear much in the U.S., probably because we think about homelessness primarily in terms of adults or teens. We are not used to seeing packs of seven-year-olds running around at night, which is common in parts of Latin America and other developing countries around the world. I did find it interesting, however, that even the term "street urchin" is derived from the French for hedgehog, which relates to the idea of these homeless children being thought of as animals, and less than human.

You do not have to do part 4 unless you want to or it is explicitly asked for by me.

Part 4: Cultural/ Critical context: (If you know more about the cultural context of a story, it can add to a deeper understanding of the work; you don't always need to know the cultural context to appreciate a work of literature, however.)

Given the cultural context of………………….., I would also say……………………………..

Given the context of Latin America's history of colonialism, I would say that this story echoes the nameless faces of the colonized, who were othered and stripped of their identities. A minor form of this occurs even when the boy is beaten by the authorities for stealing a pastry, which is exactly when he loses the dog and consequently his brief, yet comforting, identity.

Personal connection: Can you relate the theme of this story to your own life experience, other works of art or other ideas you have thought about? This can be short and brief.

Thematic connections: The theme of the story is usually whatever happens to the abstract symbol at the end. In this case, what happens to the dog (identity)? It's lost, so the theme is loss of identity. Ask yourself where else you have seen or experienced this theme.

The theme of………………..in this story, also reminds me of………………………………

This theme of loss of identity in this story also reminds me of when I lost my first dog. My grandparents had had him since I was seven, and he died when I was 17, and had just recently moved away from home. I remember being devastated because it wasn't just my dog but also a symbol of my childhood, and my family, and all of the things I had left behind when I moved away. This story also reminds me of the film, Amores Perros, where each dog in the story is symbolic of something different.

Example #2:

Here is another example of using these templates for another short story:

In the short story, "The Blue Bouquet" by Octavio Paz, he tells the story of a man who gets stopped in the street by a robber who wants to steal his blue eyes and give them to his girlfriend. In the end, the robber lets him go because he discovers that his eyes are brown and not blue.
Though there may be more than one symbol in the story, I would like to analyze the concept of "blue eyes," as a possible symbol for "uniqueness," or something that makes somebody special because of some intrinsic part about them. In the story, the robber

says he wants the blue eyes for his girlfriend because she collects them and wants to make a "bouquet" of them. This shows that the eyes have an exotic quality to them, something rare, like a butterfly, to be collected. The robber says about the blue eyes, for example, "...around here they are hard to find," which on a literal level means people with blue eyes, but on a symbolic level, he is also talking about somebody with something unique, and not like everyone else in town. The last time the blue eyes are mentioned is when the robber looks closely at the narrator's eyes, and says, "All Right, they are not blue. Beat it!" Here again on a literal level, he's saying his eyes aren't blue, so he can go, but metaphorically, he's saying, you are not unique, after all, you are just like us and therefore nothing to be prized or collected.

In looking at the title, "The Blue Bouquet," it is, of course, talking literally about how the robber's girlfriend wants to make a bouquet of blue eyes, but a bouquet has a connotation of beauty, so it seems that this means she finds blue eyes beautiful. In addition, blue has a connotation of sadness, so it's almost as if she finds beauty in blue eyes or metaphorically in sad unique visions if we look at eyes as also having the connotation of vision. This almost seems metatextual in a way, as this short story itself is kind of a sad unique vision.

Given the context of Latin American literature, one could also see the blue eyes as being the eyes of the European or North American colonizer, since finding blue eyes is comparatively rare in Mexico. In this context, Paz could be talking about a kind of reverse colonization in which the working class (field machete wielding) brown eyed-Mexican is trying to colonize the narrator "on a whim" for his girlfriend, thus highlighting the cruelty of colonization. The colonizers, after all, took from the Indigenous population whatever they wanted or found "unique" without any regard for the suffering of the Other.

Finally, the theme of the story is about being threatened for having something unique about you, it also makes me think about big game hunters and people who collect things without regard to the suffering it creates for others. It also makes me think of Rudolf the red-nosed reindeer, and how he was mocked because of the uniqueness of his nose. In fact, isn't most racism and sexism based on people being mistreated as "other" because they possess something that is perceived as unique, whether seen as negative or positive?

The purpose of this assignment is to give you a technique to understand how media bias works, and whether or not the media source you are looking at is biased toward one political side or another.

Selection of topics. First of all, don't forget that selecting a topic itself for discussion is important since some news outlets will not even cover issues that are too controversial or that challenge the status quo.

Framing of the issue: The next thing to look for is how an issue is framed and what KEY TERMS are used in framing it.

Key terms frequently have a negative or positive connotation, depending on one's political affiliation. "Obamacare," for example, has a negative connotation for those who oppose it, and a more positive connotation for those who support it.

Identify who the Power Players are, what they want and why. Politics is about a struggle for power, so it is important to know who is fighting for what power, what they want, and why. For some issues, such as Democrat vs. Republican, figuring out what each side wants and why is pretty simple. For other more complex issues, such as what is going on in Syria, it will take research to figure out who the leaders are, and who they are aligned with internationally in terms of such things as countries, corporations, tribal, and religious leaders. But once you've figured that out, detecting the bias of the news is the same process.

Figure out whose side the media is on by looking at whose point of view is the story told from, how much attention is given to both sides, and ultimately whose side does the media want to win and why. Who gets the last word?

For each article given, answer each of the following in complete sentences:

News Source:

Title of Article:

Could the choice of covering this subject be political in some way? How?

    2) Is there a bias in the title of the article that supports one side or the other? Explain.

    3) What are the key words being used and do they have negative or positive connotations, according to the article? Explain.

    4) Who are the power players inside the story, what do they want, and why do you say this?

5) Whose side is the article on and why? Who gets more time? Who gets the last word?

6) If the article is fair and accurate to all the power players involved, it is more unbiased in its coverage. On a scale of 1 to 5, what would you give this article if 5 was completely dialectical, and 1 is pure dichotomous propaganda.

7) Is there a way the article could have been more dialectical? How?

Choose 1 haiku from your handout and write an explanation of it.

An explication is a line by line analysis of a poem, paying attention to both the literal and connotative meaning of the words. Please use the following example as an outline for your own. I have put in bold phrases I want you to steal in writing your own work as they will help your writing to sound smooth, and academic.

In the haiku, "Broken Bowl" by Penny Harter, she writes:
broken bowl
the pieces
still rocking

On a literal level, I enjoyed this image of a bowl freshly fallen and still in motion, and I admire her use of language to create such a vivid picture in so few words. In the first line, "broken bowl,/" I feel broken can be used both as something physical that is broken, but also perhaps something emotional as well. The word "Bowl," for example, invokes something that is used to hold other things, a container, so maybe this could suggest emotions not being contained. In the second line, "the pieces/" again means literally the pieces of the bowl, but pieces can also be read in light of the metaphorical heart being broken and left in pieces. In the last line, "still rocking," I feel as if the speaker may "still" be reeling from some emotional break. The word "still" can also mean something that isn't moving or the opposite of rocking. In this case, it can be read on two levels to re-create in words the sensation one might feel after an emotionally traumatic situation where one feels "still" because it is now over, but there is still the echo of the event "rocking" inside, the emotional fallout that remains with us.

Here are some helpful phrases to use when your first explication:

This word suggests……………………
There is a connotation of…………………..
This connotes…………………………..
This could imply………………………………
This word suggests………………………….
On another level, we can read this as……………………………

Theoretical lens:

What is theory?

A theory is a way of thinking about the world, a pair of goggles we put on in order to see how the world fits within the confines of these goggles. The better the theory, the more we can see through the goggles.

There are many different kinds of theories and each academic discipline will have their own whether scientific or social or mathematical.

In the humanities, (Literature, art, history, etc.) the primary kinds of theory you will encounter are ways of looking at texts to understand how power is working, dealing primarily with issues of Race, Class, and Gender.

Feminist theory: is a way of reading something from the point of view of a woman, and asking ourselves who is the author of this text and what it says about women and their role in the world.

Class theory: is often called Marxist theory as he was the one who wrote the book on class differences, and how people are treated differently according to class.

Race and Ethnicity theory: is a way of looking at a text from the point of view of a specific race or ethnic group in order to see what this text says about this specific group and its role in the world.

In short, these are all theories which are designed to analyze the Master Narrative in order to challenge and expose its assumptions.

These theories can be useful to a point, but like all theories, they CANNOT EXPLAIN REALITY, as it is far too complex for any single theory to encapsulate. They are like the map in cartography, only useful to a point as reality would take billions, perhaps, an infinite number of pages to describe in full as Borges once described.

So, let's go back to our fable of the tortoise and the hare and use it to examine the way in which these different theories work. As you will recall, we had a race in which the tortoise defeated a rabbit because the rabbit spent the first part of the race drinking at a local tavern.

If we were to analyze this story from a feminist perspective we might ask ourselves: Why are there no women represented in this story? Or: Why do we assume that these characters are male when, in fact, both of them could have been women? Or: Let's say the tortoise was female, then, we might ask why we couldn't write a story in which a woman
can defeat a man without the man being drunk? Etc. I know these examples may sound absurd, but this is how theory works. And, when we take into consideration how women have historically been marginalized in our society, denied voting rights, etc. these are important questions to think about in order to understand our attitudes toward women, and how they have changed over time.

It is important here to note that sometimes when individuals who have been oppressed find themselves in a position of power, they want to do the same thing to their oppressors as was done to them. E.g.: We need to keep men in the home, barefoot and pregnant and see how they like it.

And though I have met women who share this view, the majority of women I meet simply want equality and fairness.

But one of the primary strategies of the Master Narrative has been to take the most extreme cases of any Counter Narrative and try to say that Feminism isn't about equality, but a radical movement that wants to castrate all men and make them wear pink. This is where we get terms like Feminazis, Communists, and Black supremacists.

I'm not saying that these views don't exist, they do, but they're only one small faction of larger movements who are looking for equality and fairness.

If we're going to analyze this story from a class perspective, we would look at these interpretations: Given that the hare is a symbol of the ruling class and the tortoise the worker (proletariat), then we have a fable showing how the solidarity of the working class will eventually defeat the ruling class through its steady struggle for equality. The hare, after all, was the one who could afford to go to the bar and drink, while the turtle continued to toil. Etc. Again, it is important to look at class differences, but, as we talked about, money isn't the answer to everything, and, isn't thinking that it is, just another way of embracing the primary value of the Master Narrative? Oops. Sorry Karl.

Finally, a racial analysis would clearly show this as white supremacy, as symbolized by the white rabbit and his oppression over the lowly green creature; but, in the end, he is overthrown by his own arrogance.

A quick and fun guide to how to understanding the world of story, symbolism and theme:

Stories have their roots in oral tradition, and oral tradition has its own set of conventions.

Most written stories are at least partly allegorical in nature.

Fable, parable, and allegory all work similarly, that is to say on a literal and symbolic level, with minor differences in convention.

The fable of the tortoise and the hare is a famous example.

Analogies work in the same way as do extended metaphors.

We can see the relationship here between each animal and their respective connotations.

Connotation:

As a writer, it is very important to understand the connotative meanings of words as well as their denotative meaning.

Most stories contain symbolic/allegorical elements.

When a symbol stands for an abstract concept, there is a relationship between what the thing is and the abstract concept it symbolizes.

Symbol:

Concrete thing:

Abstract concepts: love, hate, loyalty, life, dreams, evil, etc.

Finding the right concept takes time and isn't always easy.

The ability to do so is sometimes called abstract thinking.

Sometimes there is another clever thing that writers do and that is to write a kind of ars poetica, which is to say, they will reflect upon the process of writing in the writing itself, creating a kind of implied metaphor and meta-commentary on the act of writing itself; if you find a work of writing is boring, and you are wondering how it got published, ask yourself, "Wait is this really about the act of writing itself?" Then start to read it on two
levels and see if it works.

How to identify a symbol in a text? A symbol should be referred to by the author more than once, and there should be enough emphasis on it to make you think, Hmm, why do we keep seeing those sunglasses. It is frequently also in the title. Although many words have connotations

that does not automatically make them a symbol. Yes the room was dark, and dark can symbolize the unknown, but unless there is SPECIAL emphasis given to the darkness in the room, it just so happens to be dark and helps set the mood for the story because we pick up on the connotations.

Once you think you've found a symbol, it's time to figure out what ABSTRACT CONCEPT it might symbolize; the first thing I would do is think of a word's connotations.

Before I said connotations were the things we associate with a word, now I want to say, they are the ABSTRACT CONCEPTS we associate with a word.

Bird = freedom, beauty, fragility
Tree = Life, strength, family
Ipod = Technology, status, communication

These are all very General examples, which should become more specific as you really think and reflect about how the symbol is working in the story. What KIND of freedom? What kind of Status?

After you have come up with an abstract concept, plug it into the place of the concrete thing and see if it makes sense on both levels. What happens to the bird in the story? It gets shot by the little boy. Does it make sense to say that freedom is shot by the little boy? If it does, then you are cooking. If not, find another concept that does work on both levels, literal and symbolic. This is called symbolic or abstract thinking, and it is very important.

Finally to come up with the theme, which is what most people find annoying because they don't understand it, deeper meaning; you have to look at what happens to the symbol at the END of the story. What is the last appearance this thing makes? What does it do?   Then plug in your abstract concept, so that whatever happens to the bird, you should also be able to say it happens to freedom. Freedom is killed at the end of the story. Then, ask yourself what caused freedom to be killed at the end
of the story? This is often open to interpretation, so you have to make a smart argument using evidence from the text. In my story about the bird, the boy shot it because he didn't think he could actually hit it. So, the theme of the story is something like: Freedom is destroyed when people don't realize our full power, strength, ability.

The formula: Whatever happens to the symbol at the end happens to the abstract concept, and whatever caused this to happen to it will yield the story's theme.

Even though I'm talking about "the boy," I say "people" because themes are what make the story universal, and apply to more than just this boy.

Theme is similar to a moral in a fable like the tortoise and the hare, but the theme doesn't prescribe how to live your life; it just says this is the way life works.

Learning how to think this way is like learning a new language, so be patient with yourself, but once you do it will open up a whole new world of enjoyment of stories, movies, poetry, etc.

Symbolic things seem to happen in our lives too, and usually it's something very out of the ordinary that makes us question: Why in the hell did that just happen?
E.g.: I just ran into my ex-girlfriend who I haven't seen in ten years randomly at the mall. What does that mean? Should I get back together with her?

As in stories it is frequently difficult to figure out what, if anything, these events mean. And I find myself more and more saying, "it is what it is," so that I don't spend hours trying to figure out something that doesn't need figuring out.

Key terms for contemporary political discourse:

Politically correct (PC)
Cancel culture
Culture wars
Fake news
Identity politics

Social justice warrior (SJW)
Virtue signaling
Safe spaces
LGBTQIA+
Trans rights
Microaggressions
Gaslighting
White Privilege
Triggered
Echo chamber
Dog whistle
Woke
Snowflake
Deep state
MAGA (Make America Great Again)
Antifa
QAnon
Voter suppression
Big tech
Snowflake
Deep state
Black Lives Matter
Critical race theory
Systemic racism
Climate change denial
Defund the police
Intersectionality

Understanding history requires a grasp of various concepts and terms that frame the study and interpretation of past events and societies. Here are twenty key terms that can offer a foundational understanding:

Primary Source: Original, firsthand accounts of events or periods. Examples include letters, diaries, photographs, and official documents.

Secondary Source: Accounts or interpretations of events based on research and analysis of primary sources. Examples include history books, articles, and documentaries.

Historiography: The study of how history is researched and written, including differing interpretations of events.

Chronology: The arrangement of events in the order in which they occurred in time.

Causation: The principle that everything has a cause, often used to explore the reasons behind historical events.

Continuity and Change: Examining what has stayed the same and what has changed over time.

Empire: A major political unit having a territory of great extent or a number of territories or peoples under a single sovereign authority.

Civilization: Highly organized societies with complex institutions and cultures.

Cultural Diffusion: The spread of cultural beliefs, practices, and social activities from one group to another.

Diaspora: The dispersion of a people from their original homeland.

Feudalism: A hierarchical system often used during the Middle Ages where land was owned by lords who offered protection to vassals in exchange for service.

Nationalism: A strong identification with and loyalty to one's nation, often excluding the interests of other nations.

Colonialism: The practice of acquiring control over another country, occupying it with settlers, and exploiting it economically.

Industrial Revolution: The period in which there was a shift from agrarian economies based on farming and craftsmanship to industrial economies based on factories and mechanized industry.

Enlightenment: A cultural and intellectual movement of the late 17th and 18th centuries emphasizing reason and individual rights over tradition.

Cold War: The state of political tension and military rivalry between the Soviet Union and its allies, and the United States and its allies, after World War II.

Reformation: A movement in the 16th century aimed at reforming the Roman Catholic Church, leading to the establishment of Protestant churches.

Renaissance: A cultural movement in Europe from the 14th to the 17th century, marking the period of transition from the Middle Ages to Modernity, characterized by a renewed interest in Classical art, architecture, literature, and learning.

Totalitarianism: A form of government where the state holds total authority over society and seeks to control all aspects of public and private life.

Globalization: The process by which businesses, ideas, and cultures are spread and integrated on a global scale.

These terms represent just a fraction of the concepts historians use to understand and interpret the past, but they offer a solid starting point for anyone delving into the study of history.

Becoming an online entrepreneur involves navigating the digital landscape and leveraging various tools, techniques, and strategies. Here are twenty key terms to understand:

E-commerce: The act of buying and selling goods and services over the internet.

Dropshipping: A retail fulfillment method where a store doesn't keep products in stock. Instead, when a product is sold, it's purchased from a third party and shipped directly to the customer.

Affiliate Marketing: A type of performance-based marketing where a business rewards external partners (affiliates) for generating traffic or sales through the affiliate's marketing efforts.

Search Engine Optimization (SEO): The process of optimizing online content to rank higher in search engine results pages, aiming to increase website visibility and traffic.

Pay-per-click (PPC): An online advertising model where advertisers pay a fee each time their ad is clicked. Common platforms include Google Ads and Bing Ads.

Digital Product: Any product that's stored, delivered, and used in its electronic format, like e-books, online courses, or software.

Landing Page: A standalone web page created specifically for marketing or advertising campaigns, where visitors "land" after clicking on a link.

Conversion Rate: The percentage of visitors who complete a desired action on a website, like making a purchase or signing up for a newsletter.

Email Marketing: Using email to promote products or services, nurture leads, and maintain a relationship with customers.

Web Hosting: A service that allows individuals or businesses to post a website or web page onto the internet.

Content Management System (CMS): A software that allows users to create, modify, and manage digital content, typically without needing deep technical knowledge. Examples include WordPress and Joomla.

Passive Income: Earnings derived from a rental property, limited partnership, or other enterprise in which a person isn't actively involved. In the online space, it often refers to earnings from digital products, affiliate marketing, or ad revenue.

A/B Testing: A method of comparing two versions of a web page or app against each other to determine which one performs better in terms of driving conversions.

Freemium Model: A pricing strategy where a basic product or service is provided free of charge, but a premium is charged for advanced features or services.

Subscription Model: A business model where customers pay a recurring fee, typically monthly or annually, to access a product or service.

User Experience (UX): The overall experience of a person using a product, especially in terms of how easy or pleasing it is to use.

Analytics: The interpretation of data to monitor the performance of a website or app. Tools like Google Analytics provide insights into user behavior and traffic sources.

Influencer Marketing: A strategy that uses key leaders or influencers in a specific industry to promote products or services.

Virtual Assistant (VA): An independent contractor who provides administrative services to businesses while operating outside of the business's physical location.

Monetization: The process of converting an asset or any object into money or legal tender, often related to generating revenue through content, platforms, or websites.

Understanding these terms is crucial for anyone looking to start and grow an online business, as they encompass many of the strategies, models, and tools commonly used by online entrepreneurs.

Advertising is a vast field that merges creativity with strategy to promote products, services, or ideas. Here are twenty key terms essential for understanding the domain of advertising:

Advertisement (Ad): A public promotion of some product or service.

Target Audience: A specific group of people identified as the intended recipient of an advertisement or message.

Ad Campaign: A coordinated series of linked advertisements with a single idea or theme.

Branding: The marketing practice of creating a name, symbol, or design that identifies and differentiates a product from other products.

Copy: The written or textual part of an advertisement, which often provides information or calls the audience to action.

Ad Copy Testing: Evaluating the effectiveness of ad text to determine its potential impact on the target audience.

Media Buying: The process of purchasing advertising space in various media channels, such as TV, radio, print, and online platforms.

Reach: The total number of different people or households exposed, at least once, to an ad medium during a specified period.

Frequency: The number of times a target audience sees an ad in a specified period.

Impressions: The number of times an advertisement is displayed, irrespective of clicks or interactions.

Click-Through Rate (CTR): The ratio of users who click on an ad to the number of total users who view the ad (impressions).

Cost Per Click (CPC): The amount charged for each click an ad receives.

Cost Per Mille (CPM): The amount charged for every 1,000 impressions of an advertisement.

Programmatic Advertising: The automated buying and selling of online advertising targeting specific audiences.

Ad Retargeting/Remarketing: Online advertising that targets users who have previously visited a particular website but did not make a purchase or desired action.

Native Advertising: Ad content that matches the platform it's on but is labeled as "sponsored."

Ad Placement: The specific location where an ad is posted or displayed.

Demographics: Statistical data relating to the population or particular groups within it (e.g., age, gender, income).

Psychographics: Information about a person's values, attitudes, interests, and personality traits.

Unique Selling Proposition (USP): A factor or consideration presented as the reason that one product or service is different from and better than that of the competition.

A grasp of these terms can provide a solid foundation for diving deeper into the multifaceted world of advertising.

Psychology, the study of the mind and behavior, encompasses a wide range of topics and terms. Here are twenty key terms that are foundational to understanding psychology:

Cognition: The mental processes involved in acquiring knowledge, understanding, and consciousness.

Behaviorism: A theory of learning that focuses solely on observable behaviors, discounting the importance of such mental activity as thinking, wishing, and hoping.

Psychoanalysis: A therapeutic approach developed by Sigmund Freud that aims to treat mental disorders by investigating the interaction of conscious and unconscious elements in the mind.

Neurotransmitters: Chemicals that transmit signals from one neuron to another.

Cognitive Dissonance: The mental discomfort experienced by a person who holds two or more contradictory beliefs, ideas, or values.

Operant Conditioning: A method of learning that employs rewards and punishments for behavior.

Classical Conditioning (Pavlovian Conditioning): A learning process that occurs when two stimuli are repeatedly paired, such as a neutral stimulus and a response-triggering stimulus.

Humanistic Psychology: An approach to understanding human nature that emphasizes the positive potential of human beings. Notable figures include Carl Rogers and Abraham Maslow.

Defense Mechanisms: Unconscious strategies the ego uses to manage the conflict between the id and the superego.

Ego, Id, and Superego: Concepts from Freud's theory of the structure of the human psyche. The id is instinctual desires, the ego is the realistic part that mediates between the desires of the id and the super-ego, and the superego represents internalized societal and parental standards.

Attachment Theory: A theory about the importance of "attachment" in personal development, primarily focused on the bond between mothers and infants.

Social Psychology: The study of how the real, imagined, or implied presence of others influences our thoughts, feelings, and behaviors.

Heuristic: A mental shortcut that helps us make decisions and judgments quickly without having to spend a lot of time researching and analyzing information.

Self-Efficacy: Belief in one's capabilities to organize and execute the sources of action required to manage prospective situations.

Neuroplasticity: The ability of the brain to form and reorganize synaptic connections, especially in response to learning or experience.

Conformity: Adjusting one's behavior or thinking to align with the group standard.

Reinforcement: In operant conditioning, any event that strengthens the behavior it follows.

Schema: A cognitive framework or concept that helps organize and interpret information.

Maslow's Hierarchy of Needs: A motivational theory in psychology comprising a five-tier model of human needs, from physiological needs at the base to self-actualization at the top.

Dual Process Theory: The proposal that judgment and decision-making can be described as a function of two distinct processes: an intuitive, fast, automatic process, and a deliberative, slow, effortful process.

Understanding these terms provides a foundational overview of psychology's vast and diverse field, from basic concepts to more complex theories and practices.

Introduction to Philosophy

The study of philosophy invites us to embark on a captivating intellectual journey, delving into fundamental questions about the nature of reality, knowledge, morality, and existence itself. Philosophy explores the deepest recesses of human thought, seeking to unravel the mysteries of existence and to critically examine the assumptions that underpin our beliefs and values. Through rigorous inquiry, philosophical investigation challenges us to question our assumptions, broaden our perspectives, and engage in profound reflection on the nature of truth, meaning, and our place in the world. From ancient Greek philosophers to contemporary thinkers, the study of philosophy offers a rich tapestry of theories, arguments, and philosophical traditions that have shaped civilizations and continue to shape our understanding of ourselves and the universe we inhabit. It is an intellectual adventure that encourages us to think critically, explore profound concepts, and cultivate a deeper understanding of the complexities of human existence. (Open AI)

To understand philosophy, here are ten key terms that are important for grasping its concepts and ideas:

Metaphysics: The branch of philosophy that explores fundamental questions about the nature of reality, existence, and the relationship between mind and matter.

Epistemology: The study of knowledge, including how knowledge is acquired, justified, and the limits of what can be known.

Ethics: The branch of philosophy that deals with moral principles, values, and concepts, exploring questions of right and wrong, good and evil, and how individuals ought to live.

Logic: The study of valid reasoning and argumentation, focusing on the principles of correct inference and the evaluation of arguments for their soundness.

Aesthetics: The branch of philosophy concerned with the nature of beauty, art, and taste, examining questions about the nature of artistic experience and the criteria for aesthetic judgments.

Rationalism: The philosophical position that emphasizes the role of reason and rationality as the primary source of knowledge and justification.

Empiricism: The philosophical position that emphasizes the importance of sensory experience and observation in acquiring knowledge and forming beliefs.

Existentialism: A philosophical movement that focuses on individual existence, freedom, and the meaning of life, emphasizing personal responsibility and the subjective experience of individuals.

Utilitarianism: A moral and ethical theory that holds that the right course of action is the one that maximizes overall happiness or utility for the greatest number of people.

Skepticism: A philosophical position that questions or doubts the possibility of certain knowledge or claims, emphasizing the need for critical examination and evidence.

Phenomenology: A philosophical approach that focuses on the study of subjective experiences, perception, consciousness, and the ways in which individuals interpret and make sense of the world.

Pragmatism: A philosophical school of thought that emphasizes the practical consequences and usefulness of ideas, beliefs, and actions. Pragmatism places importance on problem-solving and the practical application of knowledge.

Ontology: The branch of philosophy that examines the nature of being, existence, and reality. Ontology deals with questions about the fundamental nature of entities and their relationships.

Epistemological Relativism: The belief that knowledge and truth are relative to individuals or cultures, and there are no absolute or universally valid standards for evaluating knowledge claims.

Determinism: The philosophical position that all events, including human actions and choices, are causally determined by prior causes or conditions. Determinism suggests that free will may be an illusion.

Dualism: The philosophical theory that states there are two fundamentally distinct types of substances or entities, often applied to the mind-body problem, which deals with the relationship between the mind and the body.

Nihilism: A philosophical position that rejects or denies the existence of inherent meaning, value, or purpose in life. Nihilism often expresses skepticism toward established moral and religious beliefs.

Rationality: The ability to reason, think logically, and make sound judgments. Rationality is often considered an important aspect of decision-making and acquiring knowledge.

Ethical Relativism: The view that moral principles and values are relative to individuals, cultures, or societies, and there are no universal moral truths or objective standards.

Existential Crisis: A state of inner turmoil and questioning that arises when individuals confront the essential aspects of their existence, including the meaning of life, freedom, mortality, and personal identity.

Dialectic: A method of reasoning or argumentation that involves a dialogue or debate between opposing viewpoints in order to reach a deeper understanding or truth.

Empirical: Based on or derived from observation and experience rather than abstract reasoning or speculation. Empirical evidence is gathered through direct observation or experimentation.

Social Contract: A theoretical agreement or understanding among individuals in society in which they give up certain rights or freedoms in exchange for social order and protection.

Objectivity: The quality of being objective, i.e., unbiased and impartial, in assessing and evaluating knowledge, beliefs, or judgments. Objectivity aims to minimize personal biases and emotions.

Axiom: A self-evident truth or principle that serves as a foundation for reasoning and logical deduction. Axioms are considered to be universally accepted and not requiring proof.

Absurdism: A philosophical belief that human existence is inherently meaningless, irrational, and without purpose, but individuals have the freedom to create their own meaning and purpose.

Feminism: A social and political movement that advocates for equal rights, opportunities, and representation for all genders. Feminist philosophy examines gender-related issues and critiques social and cultural norms.

Phenomenology: A philosophical approach that focuses on the study of subjective experiences, perception, consciousness, and the ways in which individuals interpret and make sense of the world.

Utilitarianism: A moral and ethical theory that holds that the right course of action is the one that maximizes overall happiness or utility for the greatest number of people.

Postmodernism: A philosophical and cultural movement that challenges traditional concepts of truth, reason, and objective reality. Postmodernism emphasizes the relativity of knowledge, the importance of language, and the influence of power structures.

Assignment ideas:

Write an email to a company that sells B.S. and explain why you would be a perfect salesperson.

Write 3 original memes from classic templates

Have Chat GPT write a paragraph introduction for a topic, and make it better by giving more specificity.

Write a letter from the heart to somebody you admire, letting them know you you feel, even if you never send it.

Compose a metaphor of your childhood by first outlining characteristics that comprised it, then asking yourself, "What else is like that in the world?"

Write an advertisement for an ordinary pencil that makes people want to buy it.

Deconstruct a stereotype to show how it breaks down upon further scrutiny.

Think of a subject you know well, and give five key words a beginner would need to know to understand it, then 5 more intermediate or advanced words.

Write a 30 second speech on why somebody should believe X

Write a short anecdote about a time you were………………………

List out the pros and cons of something you are trying to make a decision about

Outline the key points of an argument

Find something interesting about a subject that generally bores people

Write a persuasive essay about………………………..where you are able to make up fake facts, statistics, and experts.

Look at a complex argument, and figure out what information one would need to know in order to agree with it.

Describe a meme, then break down what it is arguing for and what reasoning it is giving

Actively watch a video on a subject, take notes, write down questions, and reflect on what you learned and what you still don't know

Fact check something in the media using politfact and snopes

Fact check a popular Tik Tok video or youtube short

Made in United States
Troutdale, OR
09/26/2023